CW01371770

Signed Sealed Destroyed
One of the Post Office 39

Scott Darlington

A warts and all account from one of the first 39 victims of the Post Office scandal to have their convictions overturned. Overturned on the basis that there had been an abuse of the legal process on two grounds: that a fair trial was impossible and that it was an affront to public conscience for the appellants to have even faced prosecution.

Signed Sealed Destroyed
© 2025 Scott Darlington

All rights reserved. No part of this publication may be reproduced, stored in a retrieval system, or transmitted in any form or by any means — electronic, mechanical, digital, photocopying, recording, or otherwise — without the prior written permission of the publisher, except in the case of brief quotations used in reviews or critical articles.

Published by Insect Orange Press
ISBN: 978-1-0369-2132-3

Cover design by Kitty Behan-Darlington
Printed in the United Kingdom

This is a work of nonfiction based on real events. Every effort has been made to ensure accuracy. Names, dates, and events are presented to the best of the author's knowledge. Any errors are the responsibility of the author.

First edition

Disclaimer

This book is based on my personal experiences, observations and publicly available information regarding the Post Office Horizon scandal. Every effort has been made to ensure accuracy, but some details are based on personal recollections and may not fully reflect all perspectives.

The views expressed in this book are my own and are not intended to defame, misrepresent or cause harm to any individuals or organisations. Statements regarding Post Office Ltd, its employees, legal representatives, investigators or third-party entities are based on court judgments, public inquiry findings and my own direct experiences.

No allegations of criminal wrongdoing are made unless they have been proven in a court of law. Any references to misconduct, negligence, or systemic failures should be interpreted as personal opinion based on available evidence rather than as established legal fact in all instances. Readers are encouraged to review official sources, including Court of Appeal judgments and the ongoing public inquiry for further details.

This book is not intended to provide legal, financial or professional opinion. Readers should seek independent verification and consult the relevant experts where necessary.

If any individual or organisation believes a statement in this book is inaccurate or misleading, I welcome documented evidence so that corrections can be made, if necessary.

© [2025] Scott Darlington. All rights reserved.

The entire contents of this book are legally privileged, without prejudice and contain both contemporaneous and exculpatory documentation!

The opinions expressed in this book are based entirely on my own personal experience, but I believe I can safely say at least another 554 victims of this scandal are bound to feel rather similar.

The Post Office tried to achieve their aim, through a sustained campaign of non-disclosure, document shredding, misrepresentation, the deliberate ignoring of facts, spending vast amounts of public money, wrongful prosecutions and, finally, chaos in the courtroom.

In doing so, the Post office committed the biggest miscarriage of justice in British legal history and, in trying to cover this up, a possible state sponsored attempt at perverting the course of justice.

Anon

For everyone who always believed I was innocent.

Thankyou

Contents

Signed Sealed Destroyed	i
Preface	1
Birth, childhood and youth	5
My 30s and the death of my mother	16
Post Office Ltd.	21
Running it all as a business	39
The slide into hell	49
The 'Audit' 12th Feb 2009	64
Here comes Crown Court	74
CCJs, bailiffs & foreclosure	89
The JFSA and Alan Bates	97
The select committee hearing	114
The GLO and the Great Rock and Roll Swindle.	119
The Settlement agreement.	145
The Empty Promise of Justice	155
Big Money always seems to sour things.	159
Convictions are overturned.	166
Starting all over again.	171
The public inquiry.	175
Bates v The Post Office	196
The heroes	204

Preface

My name is Scott Darlington, I am now aged 62.

I never planned to write a book. I certainly never imagined being part of the biggest miscarriage of justice in British legal history.

But when you've lived through all that we did, the accusations, the isolation, the wreckage - well, silence just feels like complicity.

This book isn't just a memoir. It's a testimony. A warning. I wanted to record what happened, not just to me, but to so many others, in plain terms and no apologies for telling it straight.

In February 2010, at Chester Crown Court, I was convicted of five counts of false accounting in connection with the Post Office IT scandal. A conviction that completely upended my life in every way imaginable.

Writing this book is my attempt to find some sense of liberation from the destruction it caused. Physically, emotionally, financially and psychologically.

Signed Sealed Destroyed

I was sentenced to 3 months in prison, suspended for 2 years, £410 costs and 110 hours of community service.

This is a tale of an ordinary citizen like me getting caught up with two of the most egregious, duplicitous dreadful organisations. A public corporation and certain areas of the UK legal system. What I experienced at the hands of the Post Office felt indistinguishable from what you'd expect from a criminal organisation. Entirely based on 'group think' and pure personal greed, the type of people that populate these organisations are the worst I have ever encountered in my whole life. There are, of course, quite a few exceptions and they know who they are, but from my own 16-year experience, vanishingly few.

A period of time that has completely devastated my life in every aspect. I will never be repaired. I can only try to be the best version of me as I am now, I will never be the old me ever again. All those pesky new synapses mean there is no return. Worst of all, it was all so unnecessary.

Signed Sealed Destroyed

I have always been a happy go lucky kind of character, never taking life too seriously, kind of on the sunny side of things. I seem to be known for my dark sense of humour and comedic use of the inappropriate timing of my comments! I've generally been very optimistic and always thought my future would be bright.

I had been involved in writing and performing my own music for many years, with its associated sporadic income, when I got to a point in my life as a new father, I needed to try and really improve things financially for the sake of my family.

I decided I wanted to buy a business, preferably a food business. What I eventually bought ended up poisoning my life and many, many others. I mean complete destruction.

I only bought a post office for what I thought was going to be stability, a decent regular income, a new direction and an opportunity to refurbish and improve the current business.

I wasn't particularly attracted by the 'community service' aspect though I didn't mind if that was going to be the case. Little did I know the very thing that seemed like a new beginning would lead to a complete dismantling of my steady life. Loss of income, loss of reputation, loss of trust and a complete loss of self-worth—all replaced by an excruciating fight for justice. I also lost peace, I lost so many family moments with my young daughter and any future ambition.

From the first sign of trouble right up to today, my life has been dominated by ever increasing anxiety. The enormous legal challenge has undoubtably been overwhelming.

What was eventually uncovered may leave you in disbelief. From the joke of corporate employees to a greedy, nasty, legal system.

1

Birth, childhood and youth

I was born 16th of June 1962 in Macclesfield, Cheshire at home, on a plastic red sofa, in a council flat. Try not to picture the scene.

My father, Ron, who is still alive, god bless him, was a mechanical engineer at the time and my mother, Jean, was a traditional housewife looking after myself and my older brother Steve. When I was aged two my family moved to a brand-new council house on an estate that was full of young families of a similar age.

I can safely say I had a naive childhood. Blissfully ignorant of the nasty things in life or any worry. My mum and dad were both really nice people. Mum was really caring and kind and didn't have a bad word for anyone. She was a popular, friendly lady, outgoing and known for her beaming smile. My dad is also a very friendly person, definitely on the extrovert side. He's a good talker, but not always the best listener! He is a fair-minded man and politically left of centre.

I got on really well with my brother and we regularly played football, usually myself and dad versus Steve, and a bit of chess together. We also both have a very similar sense of humour and a mutual interest in music. We spent hours taking turns with the record player listening to each other's favourites. I would force him to listen to Slade and The Sweet and he would play me Emerson, Lake and Palmer, Genesis and psychedelic rock band, Gong. Great memories. If I listen to any of that music today, it takes me right back.

Steve, being 3 years older than me, had a different set of friends to mine but we all seemed to mix well. School summer holidays were spent playing football with him and my dad, riding around with friends on a hand-me-down pushbike, pitch and putt golf in the local park, playing with matches, throwing stones, shooting air pistols, climbing trees, building secret dens in hedgerows, blood capsules, cap guns, itching powder and stink bombs thrown into the old telephone box. Ha-ha, terrible really! A proper 1960's childhood.

The estate I lived on was my whole world looking back. It had a large play area for kids with large concrete and wooden structures to play on. A castle, a boat, a maze and an aeroplane. The boat was particularly dangerous; solid concrete and surrounded with actual large, jagged rocks embedded into the ground. Children were regularly slipping off them and hurting themselves, me included, but the danger was great fun for kids. The familiar sound of an ambulance arriving was very common. I loved it. I never went too far away.

By the time I was aged 9, my dad had turned professional as a cabaret entertainer. This was in the early 1970's, the heyday of that kind of entertainment. He had grown up as a brass band cornet player and somehow re-invented himself into a vocalist/instrumental/comedian complete with a stage name - Jason D'arcy, his real name being Ron Darlington! This meant we didn't see as much of him anymore. He was always off to work at night and was away often, taking his act to clubs in Bristol and Birmingham and three years of summer seasons in Blackpool. He worked with all the great names from those days. Freddie Starr, Frank Carson, Ken Dodd, Bernard Manning, the list is long. He was in Blackpool for 6 months at a time and had a flat there very close to Bloomfield Road, Blackpool's football stadium. I can remember his bed folding up into the wall, which I thought was fantastic. So almost every weekend and school holidays, my mum would take us to go to stay with him. Steve and I would ride up and down in the trams and go to Blackpool tower ballroom to watch

Reginald Dixon playing the organ to a completely empty room. We would get some pocket money to spend, but as you can imagine this lasted about thirty seconds.

When my dad was away, I missed him terribly and would always burst in to tears having to say goodbye to him. Because of my dad's absence I grew closer to my mum, of course. We always had a nice time together: I remember baking cakes with her and playing 'cats cradle' with a loop of string for hours on end. We listened to a lot of music together; she really was lovely. As a child I had blond hair, and I would get my mum to blow dry it to resemble the lead singer of the band Sweet! Ahh simpler times.

I remember there was always some kind of music in the house. My dad practicing his trumpet and rehearsing his vocals for his shows and sheet music for Stevie Wonder, Billy Joel and Barry Manilow songs spread across the sofa along with his promotional photos in boxes. My brother Steve became interested in learning to play Saxophone and developed a mutual interest in Jazz with my dad. It was perfectly normal to hear my dad singing through his material in the dining room and my brother playing sax and Jazz records upstairs. I never took to Jazz at all and was more interested in Glam Rock, a teenage rampage was beckoning.

Signed Sealed Destroyed

One time in Blackpool I discovered an acoustic guitar in my dad's flat. There was a chord book with it, and inside it had pictures of where the fingers should go on the guitar. As a result of this discovery, I started to teach myself from this book. It was slow progress but later on, aged 18 and not particularly good, I was in my first band. I became hooked with making a loud noise and have been involved with music ever since.

My dad took me to Old Trafford quite a few times to watch Man Utd during The Tommy Doherty era. I even saw George Best, Bobby Charlton and Dennis Law play at Pat Crerand's testimonial. I remember the atmosphere at Old Trafford being absolutely incredible that night.

But apart from kicking a ball about with me, my dad didn't pay much attention to my interests and rarely attended any school events or any of my future gigs. I couldn't really understand it but eventually I just accepted it. He's a really good man, it was just different times, I suppose. I do remember my mum being the opposite, she was always there for my school and sports events.

My brother Steve is far more academic than myself and achieved a place at Grammar school. This was a big deal for my family, but I attended a comprehensive school which set us on very different trajectories through life. My school was very much like the film 'Kes'. Broken Cross secondary modern, an all-boys school with very basic facilities and teachers who liked a drink at lunchtime. Corporal punishment was around then, and my school employed the cane and the slipper! The cane was saved for the worst offences and it was kept on the wall of the headteachers office. My favourite teacher, Mr Spence, used to give us cigarettes, we smoked them whilst hiding behind a big tree on the school fields. I kid you not.

Although I was in the top class, there was a very big drop off below this. A lot of the 'lower' classes were full of kids we now know as children with special educational needs and disabilities. At the time they were not treated as such and were just considered to be on, what comedian Pete Kay called, the 'thick table'. There were 50 pupils in my class; I remember this because I came 50th for religious education!

While at home, Steve would be reading the Financial Times aged 15. As I said we were on very different academic trajectories. Still, I really enjoyed my time at school, was lucky to avoid the 'thick table' and stayed in the top class throughout my schooldays.

Signed Sealed Destroyed

I was an above average academic but treated the whole experience as a laugh and a joke. I really could have done a lot better, and this was something I would come to regret later in life. I joined the trampolining team and incredibly, I became Cheshire champion for my age group. I loved trampolining and carried on training all through my school days. I have never been as fit as I was then, that's for sure.

On leaving school with a few O-levels I had absolutely zero idea of what I wanted to do. Comprehensive education did nothing to prepare kids for the world of work, we didn't have a 6th form, and I was unaware of the possibility of attending college or other further education. I distinctly remember my one and only careers lesson recommending I try for either a 'petrol pump attendant' or 'joining the Army'. Jesus Christ. So, the thought of obtaining work terrified me no end and gave me my first bout of work anxiety. I just didn't know what I wanted to do. I hadn't been exposed or introduced to anything by anyone. Things are drastically different today, thankfully.

My dad became fed up with me loitering at home and hassled me to write to local firms. Despite me opting out of metalwork at school, and to everybody's surprise, I was offered an apprenticeship in mechanical engineering at ICI Pharmaceuticals division based in Macclesfield. This was considered a plum job with a top end company, and it was. Unfortunately, I hadn't grown up and this seemed an extension of school so I treated this as I did school, a laugh and a joke and didn't take it too seriously, much to my employer's frustration at times. I was always chuckling instead of learning.

Looking back, I had imposter syndrome and always thought I was a fish out of water. Not really a proper apprentice engineer, just winging it. Anyway, I finished my four-year apprenticeship, and aged 20, qualified as a mechanical engineer and worked there for 3 more years maintaining high speed tablet packaging machinery until I was introduced to the prospect of travelling by some friends who were doing just that. I knew I could stay at ICI for the rest of my working life, it was a well-paid job and great conditions to work in, but I fancied Inter-railing through Europe for a month, then lots more adventures. I decided that if I don't do it now, I might never do it.

So aged 23, I left ICI. This was a big decision of course. The day I handed my notice in; my boss Steve Foster caught me arriving a couple of minutes late for work and gave me a ticking off. When I went to see him to actually hand in my notice, he thought I was handing it in because he had bollocked me earlier! We had a long chat, and he admitted that he wished he had tried a few adventures before settling down.

My girlfriend, Donna, also left her job and together we both inter-railed through Europe for a month, camping the whole time. We were so naive, the tent we took was too heavy, we only had a basic idea of where we wanted to go, and I also carried a guitar everywhere as well. We weaved our way through Europe taking in Paris, Geneva, Zurich, Luxembourg, Munich, Innsbruck, Rome, Venice, across into what was then Yugoslavia, then finally Athens where we took a ferry to Israel and spent a year there.

We worked on a Kibbutz in the Golan Heights near the Lebanese border. If you are unaware what a kibbutz is, it is a community all living and working for the good of the kibbutz, no money is required as everything you could possibly need and want is provided. Clothes, all food, the accommodation, even beer and cigarettes. This kibbutz earned income from its avocado fields and made those classic granny tartan slippers.

We stayed there for almost 5 months before moving to Tel Aviv. I spent months busking in Tel Aviv. We both had jobs in bars and even did a bit of TV extra work. We also got to see The Stranglers in concert there. Great times.

This experience was a true life changer because it revealed fully my own free spirit. A great year for broadening my horizons.

On returning to the UK, we got a flat and moved in together. I had no interest in resuming engineering ever again. This attitude had serious financial consequences, but I wanted to try getting somewhere with my band, or at least something to do with music. The jobs I indulged in for the next 15 years never paid much, certainly nothing like the wages I was earning at ICI. I managed a record shop, worked at a small record label, worked in a tool shop and spent time on the dole.

Working at the record label was probably my favourite job I ever had. It was Hectic House records. The label owned and run exclusively by The Macc Lads. If anybody knows the band I am talking about they will appreciate the sheer mayhem this 2-year period of my life was!! Absolutely hilarious and disgraceful in equal measures. All the while I was in my own band and really trying to get somewhere. I mean really trying. Rehearsing three nights a week for quite a few years. I spent the rest of my 20's trying. This was hard work but so enjoyable.

Signed Sealed Destroyed

Here I am in my band The No-Morgans. Great times.

2

My 30s and the death of my mother

By the time I got to 32, my efforts at trying to be a rock star were just about over. Absolutely brilliant times, so many adventures and stories to tell, supporting Manic Street Preachers and Blur, lots of time spent in recording studios, regular gigs at Manchester Boardwalk, our own full time rehearsal rooms, it had really dominated my life. We eventually played our last gig, supporting Bad Manners at the George Robey in Finsbury Park London and that was it. What a ride.

But I still wanted to carry on writing songs, it's a passion that doesn't go away. So I got together a decent home studio and paid for a years' sound engineering course at The Cutting Rooms in Manchester. I loved it, I couldn't wait to get to college to learn more. I made some friends for life too. A brilliant year of music production education that I really absorbed, fantastic. I now had the skills to record music at home at a professional quality, so I wanted to pursue my songwriting full on.

I put a lot of effort into obtaining a publishing contract so

Signed Sealed Destroyed

I could do this for a living. This is what I wanted to do. For the first time in my life, I found something I really wanted to pursue, to supplement this and to avoid a day job, I also did a bit of TV extra work including Coronation Street and Hollyoakes and worked as a live stage monitor engineer at a local music venue.

Among the artists I had the pleasure of working with were Kiki Dee, Chas and Dave, Wilko Johnson, Glenn Tilbrook and Sex Pistols' bassist Glen Matlock. I loved doing this too. It became my social life. Things were ticking over quite nicely. All the time I am up until late at night writing songs. This was my life for quite a long time.

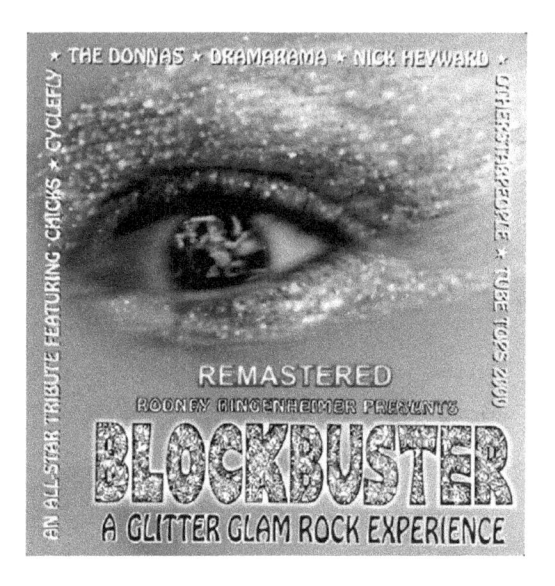

A pal of mine worked at a record label in London and managed to get us a shot at getting a track onto an album of glam rock covers over in the USA. Incredibly our cover of the brilliant Slade song Gudbuy T' Jane was selected, and it made it onto the album under the name of UKPLC. We were invited to Los Angeles for the launch party. My pal couldn't make it, so my brother Steve came with me instead. Also On this album were Nick Heyward and Clem Burke from Blondie. All put together by the legendary Los Angeles DJ Rodney Bingenheimer. We flew out to LA on the Friday, attended the launch party on the Saturday and flew back to the UK on the Sunday. Crazy! Never a dull moment.

Hitting 34 my mother was diagnosed with bladder cancer. This moment changed my life forever. It also changed me as a person forever too. Ironically, my mother ran her own cigarette vending business. I decided to take over my mother's job so she could get treatment for her cancer without her business collapsing. Nobody knew then that it would continue for 2 and a half dreadful years, obviously deteriorating continuously. This caused my first true depression. I really struggled with the possibility of my mother's death, and I felt totally lost.

My mother died at the age of 60 in 1998 and never met my only child, my daughter Kitty, a huge regret for me. The reality of the cigarette business meant, that despite the crushing grief, I had to work the very next day to keep her business going. Brutal, no time off, no time to grieve, straight back to the grind.

Over the next 18 months I suffered post-traumatic stress syndrome, resulting in me losing my hair in big circles all over my head. The years of caring for my mum and witnessing her death all came to the surface. I struggled to cope with all this, and I lost all my confidence.

Now what was I going to do?

My head now looked like a Leopard with circles of hair missing everywhere. Not the best I've ever looked! The doctor told me there was nothing he could do, so I decided to try acupuncture and Chinese medicinal herbs and go for a two-week holiday to Miami to try and reduce my stress and symptoms. I wasn't expecting anything to repair my head, it was me grasping at straws trying anything to help this ugly condition. I developed a sudden interest in hats because I felt so self-conscious about how I looked. I wasn't particularly vain, but I did feel pretty awful about this.

Incredibly, a few weeks after returning from this holiday my hair started to grow back. Whether it was the Chinese herbs I will never know, but something worked. Could be the classic placebo effect maybe, but it was a result. All my hair grew back, and this really did help me regain some confidence. I didn't feel like a walking illness anymore and even today I still love hats! Maybe those Chinese herbs aren't such a myth after all.

3

Post Office Ltd.

On 3rd October 1999, my beautiful daughter, Kitty, was born. For four years, I carried on running my mum's business while writing songs for a publisher. But the cigarette vending sector was in decline and, with a forthcoming smoking ban in pubs, my mother's business had to be sold.

After the sale my sporadic income from music and TV extra work wasn't enough to support my new responsibilities as a father. Donna and myself had bought a house so I needed a business where I could effectively "buy" an income, hit the ground running and improve it. Being a keen home galloping gourmet, I fancied something food oriented. I scoured commercial business listings for cafés, bistros, chippies, sandwich shops and delis. I even had an offer accepted on a deli, only to be gazumped at the last minute.

Then came the fateful day. I spotted an advert for a Post Office and shop in Alderley Edge, one of the wealthiest areas in Cheshire, just six miles from Macclesfield. The purchase price of the branch was £154k. The shop's retail sales turned over around £100k annually, generating around £60k profit, and the Post Office remuneration for this branch averaged £54k per year.

I spent a week parked nearby, watching the footfall. It was a busy place, but outdated and grotty inside. Surrounded by expensive shops and restaurants, it had real potential. Confident that I could modernise it, I ran the figures past my brother, Steve. I discussed this opportunity at length with Donna and we decided it was a go-er. This was a big decision to say the least. To purchase the business, we needed to take a loan out against our house, so we both knew it had to be successful for us.

May God have mercy on my soul.

I was about to step into a total effing nightmare.

Incredibly it took a year from attempting to buy this thing until I got in there. That alone should have warned me about the type of organisation and people I was about to get involved with.

Bear in mind I had absolutely no prior interest in being a postmaster whatsoever, after all I was a failed indie post punk star in my own mind. I also held that stereotype image of the dour postmaster in a brown jacket, jaded after too many years behind his counter, so this kind of future activity had certainly never crossed my tiny mind. But it was all about buying a decent income and throwing myself into it, to try and make the whole thing even better with the goal of improving everything for my family. I had initial ideas of staff running the post office side of things with me doing the refurbishing and buying quality stock for the shop side. After all, it was in the centre of a very wealthy village. Surely, I could make a success of this.

After applying for the contract to run the Post office part of the premises, Post Office Ltd conducted a very extensive look into every possible aspect of my financial background and it had to be whiter than white, blemish free. I was required to provide a detailed business plan to include how I was going to ingratiate myself within the local population, with the sole intention of increasing Post Office footfall! erm… I found this requirement quite comical.

Finally, after all this time, my application was accepted, and I was sent on a 2-week training course to a Post Office premises in Liverpool. This consisted mainly of role playing, which I hate. From memory there were 5 people like me and 3 Post Office 'trainers'. There was a row of Horizon terminals set up on a kind of dummy shop countertop. We pretended to be postmasters, and the trainers pretended to be customers.

Various transactions were gone through and the basic operation of the computer used in branches, called the Horizon system, was explained as we went along. I do remember thinking the system was a bit antiquated, but it did seem to work. We did this every day, slowly getting to know the various transactions and the associated paperwork involved. We only did one 'office balance' (a total reconciliation of all transactions) and without exception everyone was totally confused, including myself. Nothing seemed intuitive at all, but we were told not to worry as our onsite trainer would take us through it when we get into our own branch. So, I just took it for granted that it would be easier when I get to do it in a real-world situation and not with this role playing, but I wasn't totally convinced that things would make more sense in the branch.

A couple of weeks after this, I'm wondering whether I'm even doing the right thing, pondering the fact that if I take this business on, my life and responsibilities will change dramatically once the branch is transferred to me.

Do I really want this sort of responsibility?

The transfer

On transfer day, 12th March 2005, I was at the branch and representatives from the Post Office were there to give me the keys, the codes for the safe and hand me a contract to sign. I had not seen this contract before but naively presumed this would be a mature contract and would be a fair arrangement with 'Britain's most trusted brand', after all, there were over 11,000 branches in the UK. I hardly had the time to run this past a contract lawyer, did I? I was about to take over the branch and the purchase money had been transferred.

Knowing what I now know, this was a huge red flag. I should have had the opportunity to obtain legal advice. I'm not sure it would have changed my view on taking this business on because I would not have expected in a million years that the Post Office branch IT system would be so abysmal.

It may seem really naive by me, but this was how the whole transfer was structured by Post Office and seemed that 'this is the way it is'. Anyway, that was it, the branch was now my responsibility.

And I'm in

Aged 42, I gritted my teeth and thought ok, it's time to see if my original ideas could be implemented. Can I cope? Will this work? I'm not a natural businessman but I knew I could do something.

Little did I know I was now deeply involved with what turned out to be, let's be quite clear here, a criminal organisation.

Surely not, not your local post office? It can't be like that, can it?   Fasten your seatbelts…

Things didn't quite pan out like I first envisaged, in fact nowhere near my original plan. From day one, I was snowed under with customers, no easing in. I inherited the staff from the previous owner and it didn't take long to realise that despite the high turnover, I couldn't really afford to just bail out and swan around trade shows buying interesting stock for the shop yet because there wasn't enough cash bult up to cover the staff costs to allow me to. So, at first, I was compelled to be behind the counter most of the bloody time! Rock and roll!

I had gone from delusions of grandeur on stage with

smoke, dry ice and applause, to raising my voice to stone deaf old ladies.

I can assure you that operating a bloody post office is a lot more complex than you might imagine. Jesus, it was a bloody nightmare at times. The sheer number of services were mind boggling. Of course, the customers presumed I was an expert from day one.

Alderley Edge post office was not like most other 'village' post offices. It consisted of quite a large shop selling a vast range of greetings cards, a large area of office stationery, and down the centre some 'gifts' like photo frames and candles, with a 3-position counter at the rear. Behind the post office counter was a door to a storage area, an enormous safe with an electronic lock, a small area to brew tea and coffee, a small office and a toilet.

This branch was rammed out daily with local jewellers sending a lot high value stuff requiring insurance, local businesses paying in large amounts of takings, firms with fleets of company cars coming in with 200 tax disc renewals to sort out, wealthy people wiring money all over the world, very few unemployment benefit payments but a lot of pensions and sacks and sacks of general mail every single day.

This is why the remuneration to me was quite high, it was all derived from the value of the transactions carried out. Each transaction doesn't pay very much but the sheer numbers of them added up to quite a decent income.

My very first customer was a lady with 25 cheques to be deposited in a scout group National Savings account, something not covered in my training! So, from the very get go it was sinking in that I had taken something on that was going to be very taxing indeed.

From here on I was literally learning on the hoof with advice from my staff, whom I inherited from the previous owner; Trish, who had worked there for years, Arthur, a very experienced postmaster and a lovely chap called Jack who only worked on a Friday. He was 78 years old and previously had his own branch for 35 years, so they were all a fountain of knowledge.

POL did provide an on-site trainer for the first week to include training on performing my first 'office balance'. Little did I know that this weekly activity was going to be the future undoing of my life, and for so many others.

The weekly balance

This 'office balance' had to be completed on a Wednesday and consisted of 2 aspects.

1. Paperwork reconciliation

This involved sorting an enormous pile of documents generated during the week into security envelopes for clearing departments. Cheques and Girobank slips to Chesterfield, vehicle tax reconciliations to the DVLA, foreign currency returns, etc. Every figure had to match Horizon's records. Any discrepancies had to be resolved before submission.

2. Stock take & cash check

Every item in the office had to be counted and checked against Horizon's figures: stamps, foreign currency, tax discs, cash, traveller's cheques, commemorative coins, you name it. If any discrepancy arose, Horizon's figures had to be adjusted to match reality.

If they didn't match, I had to find the reason why. Usually, it was either a document on the wrong pile or two cheques stuck together, or some figures entered on the wrong line on Horizon which could be easily rectified. After all there were literally thousands of transactions every week so there was always going to be some small admin errors, and it was during the balance that this could be straightened out.

For instance, if Horizon said I had 5000 1st class stamps, but on counting them I actually had 5001, then this was adjusted to reflect the true number the branch held. This adjustment would then alter the total cash amount in the branch. It is these small adjustments that generated the discrepancies that were present every 'balance'.

All this took hours and hours after closing time every Wednesday night. The concept being that once all documentation had been reconciled and sent out and the stock adjusted to the exact figures the branch held, the system now was ready to be 'cut off' and rolled over into the next financial period.

My first balance, bearing in mind the trainer was present throughout the entire week watching over everything, showed a shortfall of just over £6. Every single transaction was overseen by my trainer and the branch was £6 down!

He shrugged his shoulders and said "Post office would be surprised if it balanced to the penny. Just put it in and see if it comes back on the next balance." I was surprised by this reasoning but not unduly worried, I just thought I and the other staff must have made some small errors that added up to this £6. Never mind, it's not a big issue in the grand scheme of things, I'm in the process of learning.

My first balance without the trainer took me until 11pm but over time I learned to take hours off balance night, by doing much of it in advance during the day. I was a bit green and had been waiting until we closed before starting to count everything in the branch, when in reality, I could count all the bulk items during the day and write it on a sheet I had designed and printed out to assist me. All I had to do then was adjust the figures on the sheet if we sold anything from these bulk items.

These figures were then ready to be compared with the figures on Horizon. I eventually I got it down to around an hour and a half after closing time. Every balance was a little out, within a tenner either up or down. I remember being around 27 quid up one time and the advice from my staff was to put it in an envelope and keep it in the safe or I could take it for myself! I thought this was strange but, hey, this was the way it has always been, so I went along with it. All the figures and bits of paper spewed out by horizon during the balance, then had to be kept in a large brown envelope and stored in my office for 2 years.

Experience showed me that the balance was almost always down with a rare few occasions when it showed a small surplus, which was usually cancelled out at the next balance. So this is how it rolled. When I was down, I always put the difference in out of the till on my retail side to ensure everything was spot on to the penny. I could then go home knowing all was good. Bearing in mind the remuneration from running the post office branch was around £54k so it was all relatively small amounts.

The nightmare of Christmas

My first Christmas, and an enormous delivery of 'Christmas stamps' arrived in the branch. I'm talking 30,000 first class stamps and similar in the other denominations. I said to my colleague, 78-year-old Jack, "This must be a mistake." He said in his booming baritone voice, "Believe me, you will sell ALL of them." Bearing in mind the population of Alderley Edge is under 10,000 I'm thinking, what had I let myself in for here?

Christmas turned out to be pure hell! Sooo outrageously busy, I had to employ another member of staff and open all 3 positions to cope with the sheer quantity of mail every single day. And Jack was right, we did sell all the Christmas stamps. Some people were very fussy about the image on the stamps. Was it religious or secular? Plenty of people were buying many hundreds each! I have nowhere near that many friends to send Xmas cards to, so I couldn't quite get my head around it.

Customers were queuing to the back of the shop with large piles of items they wanted to send all around the world. Every item took time. Did it require insurance? Did it need to be signed for? etc. To serve each customer took a long time. I could sense the frustration of everybody 'patiently' waiting for their turn.

On balance day we were slightly more money out by around 25 quid. This was really annoying because trying to find any small errors from transaction values of around £150k a month was almost impossible, and we were performing many hundreds of different transactions every single day, so it literally could be anything, and I had to keep putting this in from my shop till. At this stage I still didn't have any suspicions about the horizon system. It was clunky and slow and dated, but it did seem to work. So, I just continued to put in the cash to cover the shortfalls.

My colleague Jack who previously had his own Post office for 35 years, said "It's always frustrating but don't worry too much about it, you will get a large remuneration payment in January, just put it in and don't stress about it." He was right, it was impossible to find, and the amount was still relatively small in the scheme of things. So this is how it rolled.

Come January 2006, my remuneration for the previous December was just over £8K. God I worked hard for that, really hard. Unfortunately, but almost comically, my first tax bill was due and was calculated at £5k. What I hadn't realised was that the HMRC demand a further 50% **in advance** of the next tax bill! So there I am writing a cheque for £7.5k swallowing up almost all of the hard-earned remuneration I had just received. I laughed but I was crying inside!

Luckily my branch was directly next door to a trendy bar called 'The Bubble Room' so I marched straight in there for a couple of pints to paper over my sorrows. Over time I got to know Lee, the owner very well. Quite often he had a pint ready for me as I left work.

Transaction corrections

On occasion a message appeared on Horizon's screen showing a 'transaction correction' notice. These were generated if an error was found somewhere down the line. If for instance, a customer paid for something by cheque for say £56.35 and during reconciliation I accidentally typed £65.35, (an easy mistake to make when you are dealing with so many reconciliations), my till would appear to be down £9. If I still didn't spot what I had done, which was rare, and sent the documents to Chesterfield clearing centre, in theory, this would be detected by them and a correction posted to my screen for me to accept.

Once accepted, the figures in Horizon's cash totals would be adjusted and the £9 was 'put back' into my system. This kind of error did happen on a rare few occasions. It's not from poor vigilance, it's the simple fact that we all make small errors sometimes, especially when mentally frazzled and tired after an incredibly hectic non-stop day.

For another example, I remember hand counting £75k in notes ready to remit out of my branch to the Post Office cash centre. Cash had to be taken out of the branch at regular intervals to keep the amounts held in branch at a reasonable level for 2 reasons. The first being it's not sensible to have very high levels of cash on site for security reasons and secondly was the fact that there was not enough physical space in the main safe to hold it all.

But when it came to remittance day, it was mind numbing hand counting this amount into £1000 bundles. These bundles were then placed into special security pouches and collected by the post office cash vans. Always a nervous time as this is when post offices are at their most vulnerable.

Once my remittance had arrived at the cash centre it was recounted there and was found to contain £75,010. I had miscounted a tenner somehow. A correction notice was then sent to my screen to correct it.

So generally, this 'correction' system did seem to work well. I felt there was a safety net should any small errors like that be made.

So, as you can appreciate, this is all an enormous responsibility and any mistakes I am personally liable for, even mistakes made by my staff. The sub postmaster contract states this. The wording turned out to be crucial to all the future prosecutions and suspensions so many sub-postmasters were to endure.

The contract

This Sub Postmasters Contract, (used before 2011) states that each SPM is responsible for all losses caused through his or her negligence, carelessness or error, and for losses caused by his or her assistants.

This clause was written when everything was paper based, before the Horizon system was introduced and was never amended. It eventually took a multi-million-pound court case to unpick this contract and throw it out as onerous. Until then, it was used as the Post Office main get out every time there was a problem because it loaded all the risk onto us. Cheers. Whatever the cause, postmasters were personally liable.

This onerous liability is completely different for 'Crown' branches. These branches are run by the Post Office themselves, they employ branch managers to run them. These managers are salaried, not personally responsible. Any errors are not charged to the managers and are simply written off. It subsequently transpired that millions of pounds every year was in fact written off in the Crown branches, but not for the sub-postmasters. We were taken to the cleaners.

I never imagined for a moment that I was ever going to get into trouble with any aspect of this, because I made sure I ran the Post office side of my business as accurately and efficiently as I could on a day-to-day basis. As we all did. After all, I was liable for everything, so it was in my interest to have it running exactly right every single day.

4

Running it all as a business

Having the responsibility for a post office is a bit like being a doctor, in that every possible specimen of human being comes in. The full gamut of society. The rich, the poor, the good, the bad, the ugly and the quite tasty. I mentioned this observation to Jack and he boomed "Just be grateful you don't have to examine them" ha-ha, still makes me laugh.

Some of the more senior customers thought I was part of the government. One chap, on finding out collecting his pension now meant using a chip and pin card, said "What have you lot done, I want the old pension book back." I apologised for the change in the way he collected his pension, but he insisted it was partly my fault!

Meanwhile I have quite a large shop to run, too. My employee, the lovely Sue, was running the shop side but it's quite an operation on its own. I've run out of sympathy cards again; the pensioners are not happy. How many Christmas cards will I need? Mother's Day? Hell, this was all new to me.

I inherited a large section of general stationery products usually found in Post Offices. Fortunately, the suppliers of all the stationery had a rep who had been coming for years and knew pretty much what was needed in my branch and stocked it up on my behalf. He got it right every time, but the greeting cards bit was a constant battle.

We generally sold over 100 greeting cards every day and if someone in the village died there would be a huge demand for sympathy cards. I underestimated this aspect, for sure. I tried to work out a system to enable us to have everything we always needed. This was not easy. There were 900 individual spaces for cards, and this was quite difficult to stay on top of.

The shop was continuously inundated with sales reps attempting to persuade me to take on their range and I had also been visiting trade shows to buy small amounts from different suppliers to try in the shop. I just couldn't get it quite right.

I really enjoyed visiting the large trade shows primarily aimed at the greetings card and gift industry. Always a nice day out and armed with a small budget it was fun to buy things to try out in the shop. This is what I wanted to be doing really, not being the bloody postmaster. The gift ideas I bought always seemed to sell well but the greetings cards were hit and miss, some sold well, some not at all. I wanted the shop to be the best around, so I opted for a drastic change. I took on a deal with Gibsons cards. They would look after 90% of the entire range. They are very good quality cards, and it meant that their marketing girls would come and set everything out in the best way for this branch. They also had a barcode system that meant all my employee Sue had to do, was post the bar codes that were revealed when cards were getting low in the rack, to Gibsons and new stock would arrive the next day.

From here on we never ran out and everything looked so much better. It really took the pressure off me too. I could spend my evening with my family and not be constantly worrying about the stock levels etc.

With stationery and cards sorted, I turned to other retail opportunities. I had ideas of selling top quality gifts to the wealthy customers. Things like watches and handbags, but it didn't take long to realise that people didn't want to buy these things from the local post office, there's no kudos! They'd rather pay a lot more and get it from Harvey Nichols. So, I concentrated more on quality photo frames, candles, expensive toys, Bridge sets for the well-heeled ladies and a range of gifts for men.

This worked out well and the turnover started to increase. I even went to the New York Gift fair with my partner and my daughter and a 10k budget and bought things there that were not available in the UK. Unusual jigsaws were a particular favourite. All Very enjoyable.

Post Office interference

Despite me apparently 'owning this business' the Post Office continuously tried to insist on me implementing stupid new ideas. They wanted me to hard sell absolutely anything and everything to my regular week-in, week-out old ladies. Credit cards, Post Office's own phone contracts, savings accounts, holiday insurance, pet insurance, car insurance and credit cards. This might work to some degree in a larger town branch where it's different customers all the time, but in a village branch it's generally the same people coming in.

It became a bit of a laugh to keep asking the same customers if they want pet insurance every time they came in. They joined in with the humour of it all. Post Office were desperately trying to get in on financial services and were desperate for us to hard sell it all. Clearly the people responsible for the hard sell strategy had no clue about the actual real world.

Signed Sealed Destroyed

My first encounter with the type of people that populate corporate entities like the Post Office was a lady called Wendy wearing a badge denoting she was a 'Regional retail marketing manager'. Oh dear. She also seemed to think she was my boss. I'm all for learning new things from people who know what they are talking about, but her ideas, which probably sounded great in her office or at her colleague bonding weekends, had no bearing on actual reality. An example of a corporate 'yes man'?.. I think so.

I will give a couple of examples of this. My branch did a high volume of vehicle tax disks very month, (remember them?) Wendy, my 'marketing manager', looked at my figures and incredibly, was visibly annoyed that the branch didn't also sell a lot of the Post Office's own car insurance. I told her it was obviously too expensive because a lot of customers did take the relevant leaflets to read and apply for if they wish. She insisted I was talking nonsense, so I said, "show me how it's done then." I backed off from the counter and left her to it.

Of course, she hadn't a clue about what to do with customers who refused her marketing-speak straplines, so she resorted to queue hopping on the shop side. Who likes any of that rubbish when you are a customer in a queue? Some oik in a Post Office uniform going up and down the queue trying to force interest in their car insurance.

I actually asked a couple of my customers to do me a favour and get a proper quote from the Post Office's own car insurance and they both came back way higher figures than their current providers. A small snapshot, I agree, but it confirmed this was the probable reason for the lack of take-up with the Post Office's policy. Generally, they will only take it up if it's cheaper. On her return the following month the figures showed no improvement.

She even said, "You should ask every customer if they are going on holiday, if they say yes then you sell them holiday insurance." This is only a small example of her ideas. She was absolutely clueless about the reality of actual retail. Her ideas on hard upselling to every single person that approached the counter were truly comical.

A memorable occasion consisted of her demonstrating upselling to me. An older lady came to the counter and asked for one first class stamp. My guru asked the lady if she wanted it guaranteed next day. The lady replied, "I thought first class meant next day". Wendy didn't really know what to say. The lady asked how much the next day service was, and Wendy replied £4.30. The lady just laughed. A first-class stamp was 33p at the time.

Wendy didn't have the capacity to understand that the public were not automatons, being one herself. Truly, and on checking with her, she had never run her own business…Lol. No further assistance of this kind required thank you.

I decided she wasn't going to come behind the counter during any further visits. I'm sure she enjoyed a nice salary.

I also had to put up with 'secret shoppers'. These people came in and pretended to generally browse around before coming to the counter to ask a few questions regarding some of the saving accounts Post Office were pushing. I had to answer in a way that didn't infringe the financial services act. For instance, I couldn't say things like 'The Post Office saving account is currently the best around" I was only allowed to say that Post Office offered a saving account, and that the customer must do all their own research about it. Unless you were a bit thick, it was obvious when secret shoppers came in, so I found it quite easy to satisfy these requirements.

The pleasant side

It's difficult to say whether I was enjoying doing all this or not at this point, but on balance I probably did. After a while everybody in Alderley Edge knew me. Most people were very friendly, and things were ticking over. I was earning more than I ever had before, but I didn't have a lot of time spare. Being openly a work-shy fop, this did grate a bit and being open on Saturdays meant I only had Sunday off, and it was straight back to the grind very quickly. But I did feel that I was getting somewhere, providing a better income for my family and it did feel good that I could do this. I could manage to cope with this well enough to now refurbish the shop and try new ideas. All was ticking over quite nicely, and the situation was pretty good.

I did get around to refurbishing the shop, with new carpets and lighting, a complete facelift of the interior, far nicer greetings cards and better and unusual gift ideas from all over the world. Like I said, I went to many trade shows including the trip to the famous New York gift fair, and the customers seemed to like how things had improved.

I think I can say the staff were happy. I was not strict with any rules and regulations. They knew what was needed to be done and just got on with it without me barking orders. If anyone was a bit late or needed time to do some personal things I was totally flexible. No deductions in their wages or making them feel like they can't ask. Everybody has issues and a life, so personal circumstances can get in the

Signed Sealed Destroyed

way sometimes.

I had music playing, tea and coffee was available all day at any time and if anybody was feeling frazzled with the volume of work they could sit in my office and just get out of the way for a bit to re-group. I bought the pies and sausage rolls on a Friday, and I know they all enjoyed working for me. Nobody ever took advantage of my liberal attitude. It was a good and relaxed atmosphere; even the customers noticed and told me how much nicer it was compared to the previous owners who had a grumpy, rather unfriendly reputation. I enjoyed the fact that people felt they could hang around in the shop chatting to friends and other villagers.

We had a few celebrities in from time to time, including many footballers and cricketers. Christiano Ronaldo came in, to tax his sports car and sign autographs, stars from Coronation Street like William Roach and Samia Lonchambon were customers, as well as Una Stubbs, Denise Welsh, ex England footballer David Platt, Michael Carrick, members of New Order, well known rugby players and many others. I don't get star-struck, but it was quite refreshing seeing these stars in such ordinary circumstances.

Most were very chatty, and I struck a good relationship with the wife of football star Andy Cole. She liked to hang around until I was free just for some banter with me. A lovely lady and a quite a character. It was clear who wore the trousers in that relationship! Her husband was very quiet in comparison. All Good fun. So, all in all, despite it being a very taxing occupation, I got into the groove and quite enjoyed it.

5

The slide into hell

Having continually used computers since the 80s, mainly for music and graphics software, I was perfectly at home using them. But encountering the Horizon system was another world, a clunky, bolted on, dated world. The system ran on Windows NT, long discontinued by 2005 when I took over the branch. It looked, and was, very old fashioned and it was certainly basic compared to anything currently used around that time. It's 2008 at this point and still Windows NT.

Early 10" touch screens, a keyboard, a barcode scanner and a rather small, dated receipt printer. It's since been revealed that the Post Office had a special contract with Microsoft for them to provide updates and support just for the Post office Windows NT system!

More and more things were becoming automated through Horizon meaning less manual reconciliation and the associated reams of paperwork. On the face of it, a good thing.

Girobank cash deposits became automated through the use of a barcode on the customers deposit slips. I had quite a few local businesses that deposited quite large amounts of cash every week such as local pubs and car sales businesses. They used the Post Office instead of a bank because the banking fees were cheaper.

The previous procedure for Giro cash deposits was the customer handing over the cash with a slip they had filled in showing all the different amounts of the denominations being deposited. Various amounts in £50 notes, 20s, 10s and the coins etc. I would count them, check them off, then the total would be agreed and entered into their account number on horizon. Then I would tear this slip off and stamp the customer's paying in book stub, confirming the transaction and I would keep their slip in the till until it needed reconciling and sending off on balance day.

With no warning from the Post Office, these same customers were bringing in their deposit books with a new barcode on the slips. I had to ring the helpline to ask what the new procedure is. It turned out it was to do the same thing as before but this time I would not be keeping their slip. I just scanned the barcode entered the total into their account and gave them everything back. I called the helpline, but no-one knew how I was meant to reconcile the transactions. I queried this aspect again. "How do I check what we have taken without the slip to check it against", their reply, "we don't know". Alarm bells rang with this immediately.

We now didn't know if any future discrepancies could be down to giro deposits. Barcodes were also now also being used by customers paying money into the myriads of savings accounts the Post Office fronted up for the Bank of Ireland. Again, very little paperwork retained by the branch. I believed all of this was to cut costs by loading the risk onto me. (This was found to be exactly the situation during the later Public Inquiry.) So even more vigilance than ever became the norm from here.

The start of large discrepancies

In March 2008 I had my first large unexplained discrepancy. During the office balance, Horizon was showing that I had £1700 worth of stamps more than was actually in the branch. That number equated to over 5,000 first class stamps. Now I'm sure I have made some errors with the odd individual stamp, but there was no way on earth either myself or any of my staff would accidentally hand over the counter that number of stamps in error. Of course, we double checked and triple checked the stock again and this difference was still showing on Horizon.

I felt sick, I tried not to worry unduly. I really thought that it would come to light, and we had simply missed something somewhere.

I looked at all my paperwork regarding deliveries of stamps to this branch and I had not had any new stock since the previous balance which was showing the stamps to be correct. Horizon was now showing MORE stamps in stock than I had at the last balance!

I phoned the help line. I explained the situation in full and the reply was "how do you want to pay? Unless you have documentary evidence to show it was our error then you have to make it good, cash or cheque, or we can take it out of your remuneration over 2 payments". There was no attempt to assist me in tracing the possible cause.

Knowing what I know now I should have refused to pay anything whatsoever and really kicked up a fuss about it by demanding that it be urgently investigated by their technical department in detail. We have subsequently learned from the Public Inquiry that anybody doing that set off panic in the Post Office ants' nest. I didn't think I was in a position to do this without it risking my contract as I had never been in this situation before.

I hadn't got any documents to show why there were more stamps on my system than should be, the Post Office weren't going to investigate it at all so what could I do? I opted for two monthly payments of £850 out of my remuneration. I truly believed this error would be revealed down the line and a transaction correction issued. What a fool I was, no transaction correction was ever going to be forthcoming for this discrepancy, silly me.

I didn't discuss this with my family or anybody else.

This was the first incident that seemed like it had to be the Horizon system. What else could it be. One of my staff gone rogue, stealing large amounts of stamps? I simply knew it wasn't that. My confidence in this system suddenly fell to zero. What if next time Horizon says I'm £10k out on foreign currency or something? Do I have to just pay that? This was really worrying. It's a truly crappy interface and system, and now it didn't seem to work properly. If it could invent 5000 stamps out of nowhere, what else could it do.

Sometimes there was a disconnect between Horizon and

the Post Office's central system. This was shown as an orange line across the bottom of the screen and meant that the system was offline for tax disks, cash deposits and pension withdrawals, in fact anything that required the use of the chip and pin card, were all out of action. This could last for hours until it was remedied by the Post Office. Try explaining to a customer that they can't take out their pension until it's fixed. Of course they were very annoyed. This happened a quite few times without any explanation from the Post Office.

The system also froze at times, the dreaded blue screen, and took forever to boot back up. Around 15 minutes of the spinning egg timer. So bloody slow, very embarrassing when there is a queue of waiting customers. I was never totally convinced all the figures would be unaffected by these reboots but how could I investigate anything. There is no access to the Horizon system except for stock levels and cash figures, nothing more in depth than that.

After the reboot, messages appeared on the screen asking if I had any problems with Giro transactions. I didn't know if I did or not! If I said yes, it asked me to input the transaction numbers. Of course, I didn't have them as I had no paperwork with the transaction numbers on. So, I pressed no. The screen came back up and we could carry on. I had no idea if this was ok in the system or not.

Very worrying.

I am working so hard running this business, this is the last thing I need. This is adding to the new anxiety about this abysmal system. From here, things were about to get so much worse. Suddenly it stopped being pleasant to even be in the branch because I did not know what was going to be the outcome of the balances. Every morning, I was dreading the drive in from Macclesfield. I was wishing I had never got involved with all this.

During this very difficult period I split up with my long-term partner, and this situation just inflamed the already difficult situation between us. She thought I had not been conscientious and somehow messed up. It must have seemed like that.

Some time later I met my current partner, Donna, she wasn't fully aware of my circumstances. As things got worse for me, I explained everything to her. She has always truly believed in me. She has stayed with me and has had to put up with all the trouble that came my way. She has been a constant source of support, and I could not have coped without her.

6

The financial crash

Autumn 2008 marked the onset of the global financial crash. As many know, UK banks only guarantee up to £85,000 per account should a bank or other financial institution go bust, which posed a significant risk for the wealthy residents of Alderley Edge. This affluent area was home to famous footballers, soap stars, and young entrepreneurs, all looking to safeguard their assets.

The bank of Ireland, however, guarantees the full amount of account balances.

With the collapse of Northern Rock this triggered a tsunami of people literally queueing out of the door wanting to swap their money into Bank of Ireland accounts. Literally, millions of pounds.

One young lady came in wanting to pay 2.5 million into a bank of Ireland savings account. She had some sort of bond from Lloyds bank and the rest on her bank card.

The horizon system only goes up to £999,999 for a single

transaction, so a call to the helpline confirmed I had to do it in multiple transactions with the customer filling in multiple forms. I was praying to every god there is that this would go through correctly. Money Laundering rules meant I had to ask her the source of the funds and enter this into Horizon. She said it was her savings! This was just one customer. All the rest were transferring in the range of 60k to 350k, one after the other.

My colleague and I were double checking each other's transactions throughout, so we were satisfied we were 100% accurate, because any problem and I WILL BE LIABLE for potentially enormous amounts! This situation lasted a few days and come balance time I was literally dreading it. I was praying that all would be ok, what was the computer going to show this time?

My colleague Arthur stayed behind with me to give me some support on this one. After completing all the reconciliation and stock checking, the balance button is pressed. Then it's the rotating Windows NT egg timer for at least 10 minutes before it comes to its conclusions. There is a discrepancy. A large discrepancy,

It's over £4k in cash !!   four thousand pounds !

Oh my fucking god!

I felt the blood drain out of me. I looked at Arthur he was head in hands. He says in a foreboding tone. "This is a bomb waiting to go off now Scott"

Shit, where do we start. I check the cash, then Arthur checks the cash, we are the same, but the system says we should have £4k more.

This was a disaster. I did not know what to do. I knew there would be no assistance.

The wrong road

From what I now know, I then made a big mistake. I should have closed the branch until the Post Office looked fully into it and been a complete asshole about it until they reacted. No paying it back, nothing. Just keep my shop open and close off the counters at the back.

Instead, in a heightened state of inner panic I tried to be practical. I still believed that something must be obvious somewhere. Surely this would show up because I knew we had not made any mistakes. We were so very careful with every single transaction. So, the decision was made.

Signed Sealed Destroyed

I altered the figures so that the 4k deficit was temporarily papered over.

This would prove to be a pivotal moment in my life.

I hoped it would grant me a window of time to attempt to get to the bottom of it and allow me to continue trading the next day. The folk of Alderley Edge really relied on the branch being open. I felt the pressure.

This was a bad road to be going down and of course I knew it. But I had to get to the bottom of it and to open the following day I had no other option. I hoped it would be a temporary problem. God, this really was a scary situation now.

I had always slept easy at night knowing the figures are spot on in the branch, not anymore. This was the start of a deep personal anxiety that still persists to this day.

Now, the reason I decided to hide this unexplained loss was because of the way that the Post Office dealt with my earlier stamp discrepancy. I knew that they would, without doubt, immediately demand payment in full and certainly not investigate it on my behalf. I felt in a very weak position, and I was.

Horizon will not allow trading the next day if it hasn't been 'rolled over' into the next financial period so I was cornered into entering incorrect figures to allow me to roll over and open the next day. An awful dilemma but I was in it now.

Each balance got continually worse despite our 1000% vigilance on every transaction, absolutely no mistakes whatsoever verified by each other for every transaction, no matter its financial size. Horizon's figures bore no relation to cash in the branch. The discrepancies continued and nothing to correct them was coming down the line. Many thousands down every single balance. I'm covering the figures up every time. I couldn't ring the help line about this because it had now gone too far, into disastrous proportions. My colleague and I were simply bereft.

By this time, I was feeling ill, genuinely physically ill, and mentally exhausted. Totally worried and fully anxious about what was going to happen. Life was becoming intolerable. How the hell had I ended up in this position when I had worked so hard to make this all work and it **was** working.

I was waking up in cold sweats, the bed clothes and mattress wet through, night after night. I'm still trying to present a picture of normality in the branch and in my private life, but the truth was I was in turmoil. Every further balance had large discrepancies, and it was out of control, way out of control. Where the hell has all this money supposedly gone?

I had hoped beyond hope that some transaction corrections would come pouring in to rectify this, but I was grasping at straws. I'm facing a very difficult situation but lost as to how to deal with things without the whole roof falling in.

I was up to my neck with anxiety and was struggling to cope. I couldn't enjoy spending time with my daughter properly because I had this hanging over me, all the time, preying on every waking moment, ruining my existence. What the hell am I doing involved with this shit? This wasn't in the brochure. I was literally walking around like a zombie unable to concentrate on anything meaningful. I had never been in this mental state before and didn't know quite what was happening to me.

By Feb 2009 the total discrepancy was just over 44k. I was at my limit of being able to cope mentally, my absolute limit. No transaction corrections had arrived, not one. How was this happening every balance with nothing being picked up down the line? My previous happy go lucky carefree personality was gone, a distant memory.

I felt that I had to get the business valued in the event that it would have to be sold if this debt was enforced on me, so I got a business estate agent to come and do just that. They valued it at £185k but knew nothing of the problems I was experiencing of course.

I was always half expecting to be audited by the Post Office ever since I took on the branch, but I had not been audited once despite being told to expect annual ones and possible random ones.

Something happened to trigger one.

As I explained earlier, at times the branch had to remit excess cash out. But to maintain the payments of pensions and various other benefits the branch needed about £45k in at any one time. Horizon informed me that I was holding too much cash and I needed to remit out of the branch 50k, I couldn't do it. So, I ignored the request and within 2 days an 'auditor' was waiting on the doorstep at 8am.

I knew I was in very deep shit but thought at least

something was now going to change. I felt almost relieved that at last this was now going to come to a head and surely something would be resolved. I wouldn't need to be hiding anything anymore.

I suspected I would lose my contract, which would have caused great difficulties, but I felt sure the system would now be investigated and the cause of all the discrepancies revealed.

I was wrong. Completely wrong.

7

The 'Audit' 12th Feb 2009

The 'auditor' came into my branch at 8.30 am and asked if I had all the cash in branch that Horizon said I should have. I told him no.

I was going to be completely honest and open from the off because I knew I hadn't taken a single penny. In hindsight, I should have said absolutely nothing and not co-operated. I should have let them attempt to unravel all this themselves and possibly even kicked them out of my premises and not allowed them back in until this was fully investigated. After all I was paying the rent, not the Post Office.

But my conscience told me to be completely open, then surely the checks and balances of the legal system will come to my aid. I'm spitting out my coffee as I write this. I was so naive, and I would soon discover how wrong I was going to be. As we shall see.

The auditor closed the branch and put a notice in the window. People were peering through the window all day, knocking on it, all day. This was already humiliating. I couldn't even look to see who it was.

He made a few phone calls, and a further 'team' of auditors arrived about an hour later. The later public inquiry revealed that these 'auditors' had no training, experience or qualifications in performing real audits whatsoever.

Around 2.30pm, two other chaps arrived. Steven Bradshaw and Christopher Knight. They were the Post Office internal 'investigators'. They did no such thing.

Once again, we have learned from the public inquiry that these two individuals had no proper training, qualifications or experience at being skilled criminal investigators. Nothing. Unbelievable, but true.

Steven Bradshaw's appearance at the inquiry confirmed what a piece of work this guy is. During his day there, he faced numerous allegations of aggressive and intimidating behaviour towards sub-postmasters. He also showed little remorse for the consequences of the flawed investigations.

Christopher Knight's appearance was characterised by evasiveness and a lack of personal accountability. Both appeared to be easily moulded 'yes men'. It would become clear to me that this is the modus operandi of corporate entities. These types are employed for a reason.

For my encounter with these people, it was generally Christopher knight that was doing all the talking. The first thing he said was **"We believe you may have committed a criminal offence, you do not have to say anything. But it may harm your defence if you do not mention when questioned about something which you later rely on in court. Anything you do say may be given in evidence."**

I said I thought you had come to help!

While I was sat in my office, the 'auditors' simply conducted another office balance, a process of checking all cash and records, just as I had done. They announced my final figure, by passing me a printout showing the total shortfall and, ultimately, my debt. It stated £44,508.46

This had increased since my last balance. Something about foreign currency or travellers' cheques. Nothing made sense anymore. I just slumped in my seat. Staring at the wall. This was it. It's now official. I just felt that I had lost absolutely everything.

Signed Sealed Destroyed

We now know the people in my branch were not trained auditors, had no audit qualifications and had no idea that an audit consists of tracing and then vouching for each transaction right through to completion. Auditing is a profession, these people were pretending.

Knight and Bradshaw drove me 6 miles to Macclesfield's main Post Office. They seemed quite friendly and were just chatting with the usual small talk. On arrival they took me upstairs into a small room all set up for taped interviews. Yet this wasn't the police. What the hell was this. Knowing what I know now, I should have said nothing, absolutely zero to these phoney investigators. But me being me, I decided the best way was to co-operate fully. I'm not that naive these days, that's for sure.

They sit me down, get some folders and paperwork out and set the tape recorder running. I was dumfounded; this was like a scene from a movie.

Bradshaw said very little but was writing things down, while Knight went through some details asking me what I thought had happened. I tried to explain that we had been extremely vigilant with all transactions when suddenly his tone changed and he started raising his voice at me asking where the money really was, where I had 'put' it. Over and over again, standing up, shouting down at me. I asked him why he was shouting, and he replied saying they think I've stolen it.

I told him that no matter how many times he accused me of taking the money it wouldn't change the fact that I hadn't. He said he didn't believe me and asked what I had spent it on as he certainly believed I had taken it. I tried to explain that there is no point stealing from a business I am liable for, but they were not interested in anything I said. They didn't present any evidence at all about anything but said people are 'tempted by so much cash' in branches. I explained that I was doing ok and had never been tempted for any reason. Anything I said just fell on deaf ears.

They wanted to search my home and would get a warrant if required, so I told them they could come straight away as I have nothing to hide.

They drove me to my house, and they looked around, but they could see there were no signs of me driving a new Range Rover, or big new flat screen tv's on display etc. They were opening drawers and rummaging around going up and downstairs and it was humiliating but I knew I had done nothing wrong. The reality was I had very little at my rented home at the time, a large bean bag, my music gear and a telly. The opposite of the spoils of crime.

I asked what was going to happen next and they said the Post Office will look at my system and accounts and take my monthly envelopes for analysis. They also required full access to any bank accounts and savings accounts, for criminal investigation. They told me they had an absolute right to this access.

I was now barred from going behind the counter of the branch whilst the Post office 'legal system' ground into action. What a disaster, how on earth am I ever going to get out of this intolerable situation? I went to my house, lay on the bed and just cried my eyes out for what seemed hours, a massive emotional meltdown, built up over many months.

I was then immediately suspended by the Post Office, stripped of my income, and left to navigate the nightmare of these circumstances without any financial support. Now my current staff are running it without a manager.

They did take all my monthly envelopes that contained the reconciliation documents and balance printouts for every transaction for each month. I had my own way of double banding this stuff with elastic bands. When the Post Office returned all these envelopes to me, I could tell they had not looked at anything. My double banding was intact in every envelope. They had not inspected a single thing. Phoney investigators. Of course I smelt a rat.

Every day I'm down in the shop but I'm not allowed behind the post office counter. Customers are constantly asking why I'm not going behind the counter anymore, it was really excruciating. I really should have closed the post office counters at this point. But I needed something from the branch to even attempt to pay the rent.

It became clear that the Post Office had no intention of assisting me in this predicament, they offered to put a relief person in and give me 10% of the remuneration. This would not even cover the rent, so I told them where to go.

This was now a very difficult situation.

I managed to find someone local, who had Post office experience, to take over and pay me £1600 a month. This would stave off the rent arrears and buy a window of time to try and sell this fucking thing. It had to sell, or I would go bust; this was inevitable. Although I was trying to hold things together, I started to realise that maybe nothing would be salvageable.

This whole situation was so stressful I was permanently unwell. My mental state meant I had to lean heavily on my brother Steve for support and, of course, he obliged. I literally didn't know quite what to do next. I simply could not function rationally.

I did fully realise I should never had got involved with anything like this. I should have carried on with my previous existence scratching a living through music and just trying to better it. Buying a post office was a huge error on my part. The biggest mistake of my life.

I started people watching and feeling extremely jealous that they were not in the trouble I was in. Their lives seemed joyous and balanced. Mental illness really, though I didn't recognise it at the time. It took a long time for me to recognise it.

I thought hard work would protect me. That honesty would count for something. That a mistake would be investigated fairly. I was wrong. So, so wrong.

Advice to myself: Always stay around my kind of people. It's a life lesson for everybody as far as I'm concerned. If you venture too far away from like-minded people, you won't enjoy your life the same.

Looking back, I totally stand by this, I am dead right.

George Thompson

I decided to contact the Postmasters Union, known as the NFSP or the National Federation of sub-postmasters. I had been paying £13 a month to be a member of it.

I spoke to George Thompson who was the General Secretary. The top man. I explained that my branch had suffered shortfalls, I was suspended, and could he help? The first thing he said was "Do you have gambling problems?" I was with my brother Steve, and we could not believe what we were hearing. He was not interested whatsoever in my story and said the union would not represent me for this issue. I thought, "you bastard, you're happy to take the money though." I said I wanted a refund of every penny I had paid into the NFSP and he put the phone down. I was following him on Twitter and when I logged in, he had already blocked me. The fucking cockroach.

We know from the inquiry that the NFSP, The National Federation of Sub Postmasters, purportedly representing sub-postmasters, was entirely funded by the Post Office. This financial dependency compromised its independence, leading the NFSP to support the Post Office's stance on Horizon's reliability, often to the detriment of its members. Even at his infamous 2015 select committee appearance he was defending the behaviour of the Post Office towards the affected postmasters. What did George Thompson actually do to benefit sub-postmasters? This is certainly a mystery.

My trust in organisations was being educated. I now believe that if you scratch the surface of any organisation both large and small, you will find a nest of vipers. All hiding behind a phoney PR department. Call me cynical? I don't care. We prefer to believe this isn't the case for our own sanity.

8

Here comes Crown Court

After two excruciating months of uncertainty, I received a letter that officially screwed over my world, my contract was terminated, and I was summoned to appear at Macclesfield Magistrates. I felt the walls closing in.

The court in Macclesfield decided this case was too serious for a magistrate and that I would be transferred to Chester Crown Court. I was charged with theft and 5 counts of false accounting. I was about to enter the world of the UK legal system. Purely my personal experience, I discover it is a hard faced, money-grasping business. There are some rare diamonds in this industry as we shall see later in this adventure, but from my own experience, not many.

I was running out of money and could not afford paid legal representation (even if I could, it would have made no difference—just an enormous bill for me). So, I had to have what is known as a duty solicitor. His legal aid fee in 2010 was only £60.05 per hour. For that money, I quickly realised, he was not there to help with my case, only to guide me through the procedure. The hourly rate apparently was not enough for any actual legal help. Bearing in mind, 15 years later, today in 2025, people are expected to live on £12.21 an hour, but there we are.

He was an ok bloke and assisted with all the admin and form filling. He believed I had no choice but to plead guilty to false accounting, given the absence of clear evidence regarding the Horizon system and technically, I *had* altered the accounts.

I was definitely **not** going to plead guilty to theft, something I hadn't done, but I was assured that pleading guilty to false accounting was the only option. There is clearly something wrong with the 'justice' bit of the justice system if this was the case.

He then explains to me that me that Chester Crown Court is akin to the "Three Bears" children's story. There were three judges at Chester Crown Court: one was very strict and not sympathetic, one was a little more level-headed than that, and the third was lenient for non-violent cases. I was allotted the middle one. Can you believe this? It's an actual lottery regarding which judge you get, for something that will affect the rest of your life. All down to the whim of one judge or another on the day. This seems to be the norm. Incredible. I don't know what I was expecting, but it wasn't that.

On Wednesday 10th Feb 2010, I drove to Chester crown court with my partner, Donna, and my brother Steve. I waited in the wings for my turn. I was led in handcuffs into the cold courtroom to a bulletproof glass box and locked inside. My heart was racing and being in this box was really humiliating.

I sat there imagining all the 'proper' criminals who must have sat in this exact spot. probably murderers! I have since found out that this box was constructed for the trial of the Moors murderers. I hope I didn't sit on Myra Hindley's seat !

Everyone appeared to be present in court, except for anyone representing the Post Office. They hadn't turned up. The judge didn't seem too happy about this but simply adjourned it for another day. The Post Office cited bad weather for their nonappearance. Absolutely pathetic. I had endured many sleepless nights preparing for this.

I wonder what would have happened if I hadn't turned up?

I would have been treated entirely differently let's not pretend.

The legal game begins

Two weeks later, on Wednesday 24th Feb 2010, I was back at Chester Crown Court, supported once again by my partner Donna, and my brother Steve. I am in a consulting room with my barrister when it emerged that he had a copy of an internal Post Office document referring to their investigation of me, which stated after a full investigation of all my bank accounts, and all my personal circumstances that there is NO EVIDENCE OF THEFT.

He seemed both surprised and pleased with this and he goes to see the Post Office's 'legal team'. He returns about 10 mins later saying the Post Office have now dropped the theft charge. They were still going to charge me for theft but for us having sight of the document. Is this legal? Surely its utterly immoral. I am both relieved and at the same time annoyed that this sort of caper can even be a thing. Absolutely amazing, I had been so worried about the theft thing for months. A first insight into the dodgy tactics the Post Office will become so famous for.

I then saw my duty barrister chatting and laughing with idiot pretend investigator Christopher Knight. This made me feel sick to be honest. I knew immediately that this was a small, sickly world and simply a fee-based game to them.

We shall later see that the legal system can be an incestuous, dreadful, money-grasping business.

My barrister informs me rather flippantly that he doesn't know how this will go for me. "I can't guarantee you won't be going to prison, but I don't think so. It's possible you may get a conditional discharge". This was the first time I had even contemplated that I might be going down. I'm absolutely horrified, I cannot believe what I just heard. Prison? Me? For signing off accounts? I'm panicking inside now, Jesus Christ, what if I go to prison.

My turn comes up on the court notice board and I am once again embarrassingly led in handcuffs to the courthouse. This was a different courtroom to the previous one and this time I'm not in a glass box. Strangely, it did cross my mind that I had put six quid into the carpark machine for all day parking and I might be going to prison.

Now I'm sat there with profound inner turmoil. My whole body is tense with nervous anxiety, I can see my partner Donna and brother Steve sat down to my left. What if I go to prison right now? I'm thinking I can't do this to my daughter, she is only 8 years old. I can't have her knowing her dad is in prison. She is unaware that I'm in trouble, this is just awful. I feel nauseous and light-headed.

There seems to be quite a few people on the Post Office side. Who they all were I never found out. Smug arseholes possibly. Just a hunch.

The judge started by saying said after reading the facts of my case he wasn't even sure if any criminality had taken place and, crucially, he said he had heard about problems with the Horizon system that he wasn't privy to. (This comment came to have some consequences later on). The main issue being that if I had not made a gain from signing incorrect accounts off, in law, I cannot be guilty of false accounting. He adjourns to consult his law books. I am so nervous about what he is going to say.

We resume, in handcuffs, and he has decided that because I had received some remuneration from the Post Office during the period of discrepancies, I was technically in gain, so guilty of false accounting. He then simply asked the Post Office if they could verify the accounts for my branch. They replied that they 'believed they could'. This was good enough for the judge. Despite me waiting with bated breath to hear what the Post Office were going to reveal about the circumstances, they simply presented no evidence of anything. They were not even asked to provide any evidence.

The Judge then said that he felt he had to sentence me in a lenient light due to the circumstances of the case, so for a few brief seconds I thought I might get a conditional discharge. But no, he sentenced me to 3 months in prison suspended for 2 years and ordered me to do 110 hours community service.

This completely screwed my life over, despite not actually going inside a prison cell, which clearly was a huge relief, the repercussions on my future were going to be exactly the same. I am just coming up to 50 years old and now I have a criminal record for dishonesty. A total disaster for me and the people around me. I meet up with Donna and Steve in a state of shock and we try to debrief during the drive home to Macclesfield. It all felt quite surreal.

I didn't realise that anybody was reporting on my case from the courtroom, but news of my predicament spread like wildfire. The Macclesfield Express featured my case, complete with a long-range photo capturing my exit from Chester Crown Court, a humiliating start to my fall from grace. I've never been photogenic, but I looked like a gonk on that one.

I am also in the Manchester Evening News under the headline "POSTMASTER WHO COOKED THE

BOOKS IS SPARED JAIL". I will let you imagine the sort of online comments that this attracted!

> **Post master fixed the books to cover glitch**
>
> *Macclesfield Express, Wednesday, February 24th, 2010*

Macclesfield Express Feb 24th 2010

I am at home in floods of tears again as the repercussions of this are sinking in. This was the deepening of my journey into chronic anxiety and my descent into the pit of deep clinical depression.

So, I'm not inside jail but I still have a failing shop and rent arrears. I'm past coping with it and stopped going to the premises; total closure is inevitable, and I didn't want to get out of bed. I lost a lot of weight and was looking awful.

We did have some last-minute interest from a potential buyer of the business at a vastly reduced price of £57k but it all fell through literally the night before it was due to be sold at this large loss. Another massive blow, as it seemed that something would be salvaged to pay towards whatever the debt was going to amount to. The chap who was potentially going to purchase it sent a text the night before going ahead saying his wife had decided she didn't want to go through with it.

I was crestfallen, I had borrowed money from my partner and friends to pay one more quarter to allow this sale to scrape through and now that was lost too, with now no prospect of me paying them back. Did I have suicidal thoughts? Sometimes. Was I close to acting on them? No. But I could certainly understand why some people do. Rock bottom? Not quite.

Dreadful mental health

My 8-year-old daughter came home from school asking why her friends were saying I was in the papers. I had been protecting her from any of the details of the trouble I was in. I just made light of it to continue to keep her from the horrible truth. Going to collect her from school was something I always enjoyed, but now it felt humiliating. All the other parents were aware I had been in the newspaper pleading guilty to a crime. Nobody actually said anything to me, but I could feel the vibe. Just walking around Macclesfield town centre was an ordeal. I felt such a pariah. A bad person.

Whether people viewed me as such I don't know but I really felt it. Untrustworthy, unemployable and a parasite, like people didn't really want me around. This was a soul-destroying emotion I can assure you. It didn't go away for a long, long time.

Community service

I'm off to the probation office now to discuss my 110 hours of community service. This involved sitting in with about 20 petty criminal youths watching a PowerPoint presentation on the use of garden rotavators and strimmers.

Apparently, we were going to be maintaining churchyards and traffic roundabouts whilst wearing high vis jackets bearing the words 'Community payback'. Fuck off! Immediately I thought I've got to get out of this. I know I have to do something, but I'm not doing this.

I went to speak to my probation officer and told him my crime was only signing my name on accounts; I'm not prepared to put up with the humiliation and asked what else I can do? Thankfully, he did agree with me and offered me a place in an Oxfam charity shop, on the main street in the centre of Macclesfield but they could only accommodate me on Fridays. This meant it would take 14 weeks to complete 110 hours community service.

I can't exactly apply for jobs with this impediment, can I? So, every Friday I was on the top floor of Oxfam sorting out, photographing and listing online all manner of vinyl records. People would donate their entire collections and quite a few were pretty valuable, 70 or 80 quid. My abiding memory of this period is that Val Doonican was worth more than Jimi Hendrix!

Compared to the roundabout maintenance this was not too bad at all, so I was lucky and felt I had got off rather lightly in the scheme of things. I actually did one more Friday than I needed to because they liked me and didn't want me to leave. They were really nice people but thank

God that was over with.

I'm now actively looking for work and saw that Astra Zeneca was advertising for process engineers. Astra Zeneca was formerly ICI Pharmaceuticals; the place I served my apprenticeship. Here is a chance to get into quite well-paid work enabling me to contribute to my ex-partner for childcare and get off housing benefit etc.
I apply and get an assessment and interview at their Alderley site, I had worked here for 6 months as part of my apprenticeship, the place had changed a lot, but I felt this might give me a slight advantage.

I complete the 4-hour assessment alongside quite a few other candidates for the jobs available. I felt like I had done it well, so I was confident of proceeding to the next stage. I then get called to a desk for an informal chat with one of the HR dept from Astra Zeneca. She tells me I've done great on the assessment and asked a few details. She then asked if I had a criminal record and my heart sank. Of course I told her I had, and the circumstances around it. She seemed surprised and quite sympathetic and said I will get a letter in due course.

Around ten days later a letter from them arrived stating after a CRB check on me they were not able to offer me a

job. Pharmaceutical companies are in a category that allows them to refuse employment due to a criminal record.
I'm stumped.

What am I going to do? This was the beginning of three and a half years of unemployment. I was now living off £52.25 a week benefit. Despite the stuff we hear about in the news, believe me when I tell you it is very difficult to get any benefits. You are made to jump through many, many hoops just to get the barest subsistence allowance. £52.25 was all I was entitled to. An appalling situation and I couldn't seem to get out of it.

Every job I applied for I was turned down, clearly due to my recent criminal conviction for a dishonesty offence. This situation was excruciating for me. My daughter is at primary school, and I can barely afford to pick her up from the school. I ran out of petrol on a few occasions due to the scarcity of any cash for petrol. I went hungry quite often and any kind of socialising became impossible. This situation was intolerable, but I am in the middle of it. My mental health continuously deteriorating.

The proceeds of crime act

Only weeks after my trial, an envelope arrived from the

Post Office. It was from the now discredited legal asshat Jarnail Singh. Anybody who has followed the public inquiry will recognise this name. It was a POCA application against me, also known as a Proceeds of Crime act. It explained how despite them dropping the theft charge against me, they still believed I had been paying my mortgage through the proceeds of crime! You fucking bastards. How do you get away with this? What a ghastly industry.

My anxiety seriously worsened after I googled this and read "Proceeds of crime act applications are notoriously difficult to remove." Oh my god, what on earth is this? The Post Office were demanding the deeds to my house, the shop lease documents, my passport and my car keys. What I can say, is that I was not going to co-operate with this under any circumstances, whatever the consequences. They were going to get nothing. I decided I was going to store all these documents in a secure bank deposit box and refuse to reveal their location. Luckily, I didn't have to resort to this.

This application was designed to take everything from me as an individual, based on an accusation that had already been thrown out of court.

Fortunately, I contacted the barrister who had previously represented me in court. He was astonished. He took the POCA application back to Chester Crown Court and successfully challenged it. The judge dismissed it outright, stating that the POCA request had no chance of success and was an abuse of process. Of course, it was.

Once again, the Post Office had tried to weaponize the legal system against me, not out of necessity, but out of sheer vindictiveness. This wasn't about justice—it was about crushing me completely. The legal system is a terrible game. Only money means anything, and I was never prepared for any of this.

It is much worse than the industry that I do know, the music industry. At least the people involved in that are colourful characters, this industry is something else entirely. It seemed to be suit wearing snakes wherever I looked.

9

CCJs, bailiffs & foreclosure

It's now around September 2010 and I am in arrears with all my suppliers for the shop and I have no means to pay them. I feel more humiliation as I have to contact them all and explain the situation. Despite previously having a great relationship with them all, business is business, and they issue county court proceedings. There is nothing I can do so judgements are lodged.

While this is going on I get a parking ticket near my Branch in Alderley Edge. I applied to the council to have a special parking permit as the sub-postmaster and was told that there was a possibility I could get one. I then get a call to say that the post office branch doesn't qualify for a permit.

By this time my ticket has been passed onto to a debt collection firm. This firm call at the shop leaving a bill for the ticket + 400 quid. I go down to get this bill and return home and find they have been to my house too, amazingly, the bill has risen to £4k. Four thousand pounds.

Apparently, the cost for two visits to my premises.

I manage to get hold of the guy that has been round, and he immediately started threatening me. I am not a violent person and have never had a fight in my whole life. But this guy was the last straw, and I flipped. I invited him to come back to my house immediately where I will be waiting for him. I had a golf club ready.

This was completely irrational behaviour by me. I was mentally ill. Any thoughts regarding my own personal safety or for any consequences of this action were far from my mind, I really was quite prepared to fight this guy. He didn't come. Luckily for him, and me.

But when I woke up the following morning my car had been clamped. So I borrowed an angle grinder, removed the clamp from my car and threw it in a nearby skip. I parked my car in a place they wouldn't find it and incredibly, I never heard from him or the fucking debt firm again. Nothing

This experience taught me something valuable. Don't give in, front these people up, you must oversee the outcome. The moment you challenge this type, they don't have the skills that you are lead to believe. These companies exist purely to prey on the already downtrodden, and then to fleece them to the max. An attitude I would come across again all too clearly later in this saga. My life was lurching from bad to worse.

Closing down

The landlords of my shop premises ran out of patience with me and called me in to discuss the situation. He listened to me and really did feel sorry for me. He also said as I was getting money from the relief postmaster I was technically subletting, and this was totally not allowed, I could be in even more trouble. Shit, this situation is going from bad to worse.

Later that day, he emailed me to tell me I had seven days to get £5k together and I could walk away from the lease on the shop. In the scheme of things this was generous as they had the right to enforce the payment for the remaining four years on the lease, around £90k and the landlords were known to be ruthless.

Properties were now at stake. I still had an interest in the property I shared with the mother of my child as a family home. But this could be at stake if I can't get this money together. My brother Steve was also named on the lease which meant if there wasn't enough equity in my house then Steve's would be vulnerable too. Of course he was not very happy about this. This tested our relationship for the first time in my life. Unfriendly emails were exchanged, this was upsetting for me.

I found out that the reason the landlords were being generous about this was because the bar right next door was keen on expanding into the Post office and shop premises and had discussed this with the landlords. The landlords decided it was in their interests to just get me out with a £5k release payment and get the Bubble Room bar in so they could charge a lot more rent from them, than to chase me through bankruptcy courts for possibly years. Of course I was mightily relieved.

Still being a keen songwriter, I still had a decent home studio. The pieces of equipment were the only things of value I owned. So, I set about selling everything I had. Microphones, effects units, mixing desk, pre-amps, guitar cabs, anything I could sell. I managed to get to about £3900 and a friend chipped in the rest, with that we managed to get out of the lease and walk away.

On Friday November 12th 2010, the shop was officially foreclosed and repossessed with a closure sign on the door, and I had to go and clear it out. A very upsetting experience. I looked around and just couldn't believe everything had all collapsed to this situation. I felt I had failed. Failed everyone around me. I confess to having a few tears again whilst starting the clear out.

There were thousands of greetings cards along with glass display cabinets and the pay counter complete with till. What the hell was I going to do with all this. I tried to sell things on eBay as job lots but had no interest, so it all went to a charity shop. A bumper day for them, that's for sure. They could not believe the sheer volume I was donating to them.

So now I had no shop, no employment, no money, a criminal record and debts. But at least the houses were safe, or so I thought.

My depression and anxiety at this time was ruining me. I ended up collapsing at home in front of my brother and taken in an ambulance to hospital. We were watching snooker on the television and I just collapsed in my seat! Steve thought I was dead as my eyes were rolling in my head and I wasn't responding. I don't know how long I had been like this, but I regained consciousness and started vomiting. Bloody awful for Steve to witness and not much fun for me either.

Steve called an ambulance and paramedics arrived, did a few tests and sent me to hospital. It seems I had a Vasovagal episode brought on by stress. After quite a few hours I was eventually discharged home. Rock and roll eh?

My mental health was very poor. The housing benefit I was claiming to pay my housing rent was reduced without warning by the Conservative government and my landlady was not sympathetic. She wanted me out as soon as possible. A really unkind person, no empathy, I'm sure I won't forget this individual.

I could not find anywhere to go in such a short space of time until literally the night before I had to leave, a friend phoned me to tell me someone was looking for a lodger. Sheesh what a relief, I moved into a house share with an old music friend, my pal Joe Ashworth, it was a lifesaver! I'm aged 50 and I'm about to house share.

Arriving at Joe's house I felt a mixture of relief, shame and exhaustion. My life was now totally upside down on every level.

Joe was very supportive of my situation. Despite my terrible mental health, many, many great and hilarious times were spent with Joe. I owe him an enormous debt of gratitude; he was a real support to me. He kept me always entertained and got takes-outs for me regularly. He just about kept me sane and I cannot thank him enough for his friendship throughout the time I lived with him. He really is one of life's fantastic characters. Thrown together because of circumstances but a memorable period of my life for sure. A true friend for life

Despite Joe's great friendship, this was a very low period of my life. I was at rock bottom. Depression and anxiety at their most caustic. I could not find any employment at all. The futility of job websites and the embarrassment of regular visits to the job centre does nothing for anybody's confidence.

My daughter Kitty used to come and spend Saturdays with me, but I couldn't afford to do anything special. We just messed about in the local park, and she played with Joe's lovely daughter Nelly.

I wasn't just unemployed, I felt I was unemployable. My age and criminal record were weighing heavily. Staring out of the window, I wasn't looking at the world, I felt was looking at a future I couldn't seem to change. I was smoking cigarettes like a chimney and felt utterly trapped. Truly a bleak period for me personally.

I didn't function normally at all. Regularly crawling into bed at 5am, then sleeping in until 2pm.

I didn't even want to get up at all most days because there was little to get up for. That is how I felt. I had no money so I couldn't even take a bus to anywhere, just to get away for a few hours. I know I stopped caring about my appearance, classic symptoms of depression. I still didn't go to the doctors. I just tried to ride it out. Certainly, a mistake in hindsight.

The sensation of high-level anxiety is intense, very intense. It feels like your skin is crawling with irregular hot short breaths. Mind racing but not really thinking of anything in particular. It is very debilitating, much more than I realised.

10

The JFSA and Alan Bates

For a while I had become convinced that the Horizon system must have had something to do with this, what else could it be? There is simply no point stealing from your own post office, obviously. I hadn't, and I was certain neither had my staff. So where did the money actually go? How come my stamps total was miles out?

So, I simply googled the phrase 'Post Office Horizon system'. **Holy shit**, loads of things popped up regarding postmasters having problems all over the UK! I couldn't quite believe what I was reading. I should have done this earlier of course, but at the time I had no clue that others were also having major problems.

Until this moment, I had been plagued mentally with the thoughts that it could have been my incompetence that caused all this. Even though I was bloody sure I hadn't made the sort of mistakes that had caused discrepancies to the level of £44k. The mind still plays tricks. I had not had any indication of anything else that could have caused it. I suddenly realised that it **was not me!** Here on the screen was information saying the system has problems. This was an absolute revelation. What a moment. It really was a turning point. It was at this point that I found out that Fujitsu, the giant Japanese tech company were the designer and maintainer of the Horizon system.

There seemed to be many articles and various musings of Horizon causing problems for sub-postmasters and then I saw an article in the online publication Computer Weekly and the JFSA website. Justice For sub-postmasters Alliance. I clicked on this, and I couldn't believe it.

A man called Alan Bates was actively calling for postmasters who had had problems with Horizon to contact him. There were some example circumstances of postmasters who were suspended and prosecuted, and I realised this was describing what happened to me.

Along with my brother, we got in touch with Alan. He listened and was really understanding of my plight, told me he had heard the same story from many sub-postmasters and added me to his mailing list. By this time there had already been a few Sub-postmaster meetings at Fenney Compton village hall in Warwickshire. I would be going to the next one.

My involvement with law firms begins

In the meantime, I took my postmasters' contract to a law firm in London called Howe & Co. My brother Steve worked there as their financial controller and knew the lawyers. This was in December 2010. One of their senior lawyers flicked through the contract and basically said "They've got you by the short and curlies with this" and handed it back to me. Had they looked into this in more detail, perhaps it would have saved 15 years misery. Who knows, but in hindsight I believe it would. It's difficult to criticise anybody at that time with the lack of information, but I did feel that the three minutes I was granted was not sufficient to form that solid opinion. However, Howe & Co re-enter the frame a decade later.

I was then told that a QC (now called Kings Counsel, but at the time Queens Counsel) they knew, was prepared to take a look at it, but it would cost me £10k. This was clearly very disappointing, it was now sinking in that the costs for anything to be done were not only high, but they were at maximum piss-take level. This kind of practice would be borne out in spectacular fashion later on. It's amazing how much some people can earn whilst enjoying an evening bubble bath. I'm being facetious of course.

The next sub-postmasters meeting was in Huddersfield. I can't quite remember the date, but I believe it was around Feb 2011.

Donna and I arrived at a small village hall and there were quite a few people in attendance. My memory is that around 50 people were there. It was immediately obvious that these people were not criminals. It was mainly middle-aged and older, husband and wife combinations. I do remember Jo Hamilton doing the cakes and coffee. Jo went on to be a major name in the TV drama, along with a few others.

People were standing up and speaking about their own experiences and it was clear that we were all in a similar situation. This was a relief to hear. Bloody hell, it wasn't just me, this has affected a lot of people. Looking back, I was in a kind of daze really. This all felt a bit surreal. Alan spoke up about the small possibility of us being legally represented and fighting back and what a long road it would be, if at all.

Any legal action by us all depended on getting enough interest and raising the funding to pay a law firm to take this on. It also depended on any law firm instructed, raising ATE (after the event) insurance, to cover their costs if this legal action loses in court. They won't get this insurance unless the insurance company thinks there is a good prospect of winning the case. So, the reality is, justice depends entirely on insurance companies. This was all news to me.

We can agree right there, the actual justice bit was a secondary thing, money was the number one priority. This turned out to be exactly the case. It became solely about money. This is what the legal system is all about. Large amounts of money. Any justice is merely a side effect. Of course this is the reality, I was simply naïve.

Alan announces that a law firm called Shoosmiths were interested in getting the ball rolling. So we all applied to be represented and went from there. There was a lot of detailed documentation to fill in, and talk of further meetings regarding the potential, albeit slow progress over the next few months, but this all fizzled out when Shoosmiths could not secure the ATE funding.

They could not get insurers to believe in it enough to cover their costs. I don't know why, we never found out why they didn't believe in it, but it was a huge blow. I presume that the whole case was a complex thing to attempt to unpick and taking action against a government-owned public corporation is clearly a long shot. A terrible sinking feeling hit me, the realisation that whatever happens next, I will have to start again, from the beginning. All back to square one. This was hard to take. When was that even going to happen? if at all. Really disappointing.

I get a job at last.

November 2013 and I finally obtain employment. Three and a half years after my conviction. My application for a production technician at a firm called Senior Aerospace, lands me an interview. I am seriously nervous having been unemployed for so long. Of course, on the application form I have ticked that I have a criminal record.

Incredibly, the lady interviewing me asked about it and was astonished with my explanation. She really was interested in the fact that there were a lot of other postmasters in the same situation and were attempting to fight back.
About 10 days after this interview, I get a phone call from the employment agency overseeing my application. The lady says she wants to give me some "feedback". I feared the worst, of course. She then said that Senior Aerospace had decided to take me on. Oh my god, I was amazed. This was such a lifeline. I had become an outsider to most things in life through my predicament and this was now

going to change.
I was now hand-making bespoke parts for aircraft. What a turn up for the book. My wages enabled me to move out of my house share with Joe and rent a house. This meant my partner Donna was able to move from Leeds and move in with me. With an improvement in my mental health, I felt I had rejoined society. At last!

In the meantime, the Post Office had surprisingly offered to mediate with JFSA cases and had appointed a committee to oversee this. We now know from the inquiry that the whole thing was a total sham and was never intended to resolve anything at all. But at the time it seemed like hope. At least POL were acknowledging this issue after all.

I received a letter from the Post Office's 'People services director', Angela Van den Bogerd, stating that because I had been 'subject to a court direction', they would not be mediating with me. A 'court direction' was the Post Office own phrase meaning a criminal conviction.

I wrote and complained to the Chairman, Alice Perkins, the wife of Labour MP Jack Straw. This was someone I had not heard mentioned once throughout all this. I received a reply from Angela Van den Bogerd. Obviously intercepted by team Bogerd, it was an immediate cloud of smoke and mirrors. I was suspicious and realised immediately that things were not as they seemed. I had no idea then, that this was going to turn into the biggest conspiracy to pervert the course of justice in British legal history.

Second Sight

Through pressure from MP's and the JFSA, a forensic accountancy firm called Second Sight, had been commissioned in 2012 by the Post Office to take an independent look and investigate the issues with the Horizon system. This firm was very experienced in the forensic dissecting of accounting software and on July 8th 2013 released their interim report.

The Post Office originally expected the review to confirm Horizon's reliability.

The guys who ran this firm, Ron Warmington and Ian Henderson, were crucial to the future of the scandal. Their interim report was not favourable to Post Office.

Bugs HAD been discovered. The report said that some sub-postmasters had been wrongly held responsible for unexplained accounting shortfalls, despite evidence that technical faults could be causing discrepancies.

The Post Office went on the defensive picking up on a phrase used in the report, that Second Sight had not found any 'systemic bugs'. This was misleading and became a mantra for the Post Office.

Although Second Sight hadn't YET found bugs that affected the whole system, they HAD found bugs that had affected many individual branches. So, this wording was unfortunate and not what the report actually concluded, but the Post Office jumped on this phrase and kept repeating it as a mantra for years and years. In all their press releases and in front of select committee hearings, they simply repeated that Second Sight had not found 'systemic bugs' in Horizon.

Two more years of waiting and chronic anxiety pass by. There are further meetings with Alan who is constantly trying to keep everything together. He has meetings with MPs and government officials, but the juggernaut had stalled. Very frustrating. The feeling of helplessness persists. My partner and I are doing our best to have a nice time together, but this awful situation was always there, always poisoning things. This was the norm for us and would be for many years to come.

Publicity ramps up

One of the heroes in all of this, is the independent journalist, Nick Wallis. This guy had wind of this story for years. He started appearing on telly with information about our plight, I saw him on the One Show and various news channels. He managed to get the BBC to commission a Panorama documentary and eventually on August 17, 2015, it was aired on the BBC

New things were revealed including the possibility that Fujitsu could remotely access postmasters' computers without their permission or even their knowledge. A potential whistleblower, a Fujitsu employee called Richard Rolls confirmed how Fujitsu did this regularly. He also stated that the system was well known to have significant errors. This was a revelation, possibly a so-called 'smoking gun' moment.

Prior to the documentary's airing, the Post Office tried to suppress its broadcast. They issued threats of legal action against the BBC and the experts interviewed for the programme. There was also a conflict of interest. Alice Perkins, the chair of the Post Office at that time, also served on the BBC's executive board. Another puff of smoke and mirrors. Hmmm

Post Office had said unequivocally that remote access was impossible. We now know this was a blatant lie. Did this happen at my branch? I will never know. How could my stamps total be more than the previous balance when I had been selling them all week and not received any new deliveries?

If it had been tampered with remotely what would be the reason? Why was my cash total down so much when for all the previous years there had only been small discrepancies? Had I been a victim of remote access by people from Fujitsu?

Panorama had now got this information, and this was not going to go away. This issue was going to be a reoccurring thorn in the side of the Post Office.

Post Office suppress Second Sight

In 2015 Second Sight produced their final and more detailed report from its now two-year investigation into the Horizon system. It concluded that the Post Office had pursued prosecutions against sub-postmasters without sufficient evidence and had failed to investigate potential

IT faults.

It also found the evidence that the Post Office did have access to and could remotely alter branch accounts without the sub-postmasters' knowledge! So, they could, and did access individual branches, and alter the branch accounts using the postmasters ID, to make it appear that it was the postmaster who had done it. This directly contradicted what the Post Office had been stating for years and years.

This was fantastic news for the postmasters and was indeed the smoking gun we were all hoping for.

The Post Office had an advanced view of the report and stopped the publication, discredited and terminated Second Sights' contract on the spot, and closed the mediation scheme. They also published an 88 page rebuttal of Second Sight's conclusions.

Obviously, we now knew for sure they had definitely got something to hide.

How pitiful can they get? trying to save the reputation of the "brand" by doing that. Don't forget, the people at the top of the Post Office were the supposedly cream of the crop, top-level executives. Their decisions are apparently worth very large salary packages. We shall see what a folly this endemic perception was and for me, still is. The type of individuals at these "levels" were revealed to have very narrow skill sets and they behaved more and more reprehensible as time went on.

Their refusal to mediate was another rug pulled out from under me, and this had a further detrimental effect on my mental health. I realised I was in a state of permanent anxiety with depression coming and going in cycles. It took me a long time to realise that the continuous way I was feeling was a chronic condition. It had now become the norm, and I couldn't remember what I felt like before.

I needed medical help, but I was avoiding going to the doctors because I didn't want to have to tick a box on job applications asking if I'd ever suffered from mental health problems along with a criminal conviction. So, I just lived with it. Living with it was very hard and there was to be many, many more years of living with it.

The Post Office then offered me "a meeting with my local MP". Macclesfield's MP was Conservative David Rutley. I had previously written to him on nine occasions regarding my predicament and true to form, he had shown no interest. They never do. I didn't even respond to the Post

Office regarding this "offer".

As a side comment, the MP for Alderley Edge at the time was none other than George Osbourne and I wrote to him too. He replied with "Unfortunately, I cannot get involved with legal issues". Hopeless. What actual use are MPs to the general public? When the chips are down, they are nowhere to be seen. I believe they are only a quaint tradition. They cannot really help with anything.

All they seem to do is appear at openings of garden centres and anything else that comes with a photo opportunity. They do nothing for the homeless so what are they going to do for me? Maybe a bit cynical, but I don't care. I'm not wrong.

Slight hope

It's now 2015 and Alan Bates announced that a new law firm, who I'm going to call **'Our law firm'**, were now showing some interest in our case. By this time, the numbers of postmasters attending the JFSA meetings had grown to around 150. A senior lawyer from our law firm started attending to find out the full picture from the postmasters. He seemed very sure that something was on here. He explained the difficulties ahead and possible solutions for them, and we all felt relieved that someone was going to take it on again. Once again loads of legal paperwork and information to plough through.

The juggernaut gets going again

Our law firm announce they have found a funder called Therium who are willing to bankroll the costs of legal action. They will do this but take a hefty fee from any compensation achieved. I didn't realise that this was even a thing!

This will be in the form of a group litigation, a GLO, where many people with the same complaint act together as a group against the Post Office. At the next few meetings leaflets are distributed showing potential costs and, if successful, the potential effects on any compensation claimed.

This all seemed legit at this point. Although I did wonder who was paying for all the appearances at the meetings of our law firm's staff, because fees for senior lawyers are usually many hundreds of pounds an hour, yes an hour. They were travelling around the country to all these meetings, yet we were not paying anything.

Group Action V Post Office

Indicative Outcome Scenarios If The Group Action Succeeds

Aggregate Recovery – Pre Funder's return (Inc. damages, interest and legal costs/success fee; with estimated ATE premium deducted)	Example individual claim values	Estimated net return to individual claimants after conclusion of all claims
£0-£21m		£0
£22m	£1m	£105,263
	£500k	£52,631
	£250k	£26,316
	£100k	£10,526
	£50k	£5,263
	£25k	£2,632
	£5k	£526
	£2k	£211
£27m	£1m	£304,348
	£500k	£152,174
	£250k	£76,087
	£100k	£30,435
	£50k	£15,217
	£25k	£7,609
	£5k	£1,522
	£2k	£609
£37m	£1m	£565,667
	£500k	£283,333
	£250k	£141,667
	£100k	£56,667
	£50k	£28,333
	£25k	£14,167
	£5k	£2,833
	£2k	£1,133
£47m	£1m	£729,730
	£500k	£364,865
	£250k	£182,432
	£100k	£72,973
	£50k	£36,486
	£25k	£18,243
	£5k	£3,649
	£2k	£1,459

Note: All figures are merely estimates. There are numerous unpredictable variables that will impact on the actual net return (if any) to Claimants.

This document provided by our law firm shows that if compensation from the Post Office totalled £22 million and an individual's claim was for £1 million, after the legal and funders fees, the individual could receive £105,263 out of that, but if the total sum received from the Post Office was £47 million, then the individual claimant could receive £729,730. Remember this document as I will be returning to it later. Clearly these were estimates, as was impossible to foresee all the variables that could come into play.

At the time, I actually thought that they also wanted to help us achieve justice on a human level. So, I was happy that this juggernaut was moving forward.

We were told that if more affected postmasters got involved with the claim, the less each of us will have deducted from the compensation for the costs. Makes sense, yes? So JFSA put out more calls for postmasters affected who have not yet come forward to get involved. This number eventually rose to 555.

I had no idea that this many people were afflicted by this and later on (post litigation) this number topped 1000. How bad can this get! Utterly incredible that so many people were affected in one way or another.

The select committee hearing

On Feb 3rd 2015 a Business, Innovation and Skills (BIS) select committee was convened by the government to look into this issue. In attendance was Paula Vennells, the CEO, and her right-hand man "People services director" Angela Van Den Bogerd. Also in attendance was Second Sight's Ian Henderson and the main man, Alan Bates.

The lies told to the select committee were mind boggling. Vennells appeared to have had no clue about what she was talking about and just referred to Bogerd as soon as she was cornered.

She said there were no indications that any miscarriages of justice had taken place, despite knowing the extent of the complaints and all the known issues with Horizon. She downplayed sub-postmasters' claims and rejected Second Sight's conclusions.

This is when I started to realise that there was something wrong with these company people. Something fundamentally wrong with their personalities. Glued to a brand. They don't even speak properly. It's a special "corporate" tone, not conversational at all. A fascinating phenomenon.

It seems to transform normal speech into a vague, indirect and overly formalised way of communicating. To me, it attempts to create an illusion of expertise. Very strange. Very strange indeed. Unless they have taken lessons in this, it must be a mental condition as it is certainly not normal.

The attending MPs pushed back and tried to get some worthwhile information out of them, but none appeared to be forthcoming. Both Vennells and Van Bogered pretended they didn't understand what information Second Sight had requested from them in the most cringeworthy display.

[The link for this meeting](https://www.youtube.com/watch?v=9TVfz_xISSY)
https://www.youtube.com/watch?v=9TVfz_xISSY

Incredibly this Select Committee was dissolved in March 2015 ahead of the forthcoming general election on May 7th, as a result the committee could not complete its investigation into the Post Office and no report was produced on the matter. Absolutely useless. I wrote a scathing email to the chair of the committee Adrian Bailey, complaining that all this was ultimately useless for the suffering postmasters. What was the point of doing it if there was never going to be a single thing gained from it. I received a half-hearted apology.

Lord Arbuthnot

At around the time I started to realise the extent of Lord Arbuthnot's involvement in the scandal. James Arbuthnot was the MP for North East Hampshire from 1997 to 2015. He was first alerted to potential problems with the Horizon computer system during a coffee morning in his constituency, in 2009, when he was introduced to the former Sub-postmaster Jo Hamilton.

Arbuthnot at first attempted to raise Hamilton's case with the government, specifically the Secretary of State for Business, Peter (now Lord) Mandelson. Arbuthnot received a "frustrating" response from Mandelson's junior, Pat McFadden, effectively washing the government's hands of the Post Office business, despite being its sole shareholder.

Undeterred, Arbuthnot founded a group of MPs who also had constituents claiming they had suffered life changing problems as a result of their interactions with the Horizon IT system and the Post Office's punitive practices. They eventually found themselves, in 2012, face-to-face with Paula Vennells and other senior executives at the Post Office. None of the execs would entertain the idea that there was anything wrong with the Horizon IT system.

Paula Vennells went one further. According to the minutes of the meeting, Vennells told the MPs:

"Every case taken to prosecution that involves the Horizon system thus far has found in favour of the Post Office." This was pure smoke and mirrors.

Lord Arbuthnot has been fantastic for the Postmasters. He realised that there were serious questions to be answered and never gave up. He has done his utmost to raise the issues at the highest level. He led a cross parliamentary group, set up to investigate the issue. He is so respected by all sides in parliament he has real clout. He used it to its fullest and kept trying his utmost, constantly plugging away to help get this uncovered and sorted out.

Despite his respected high profile, he was given the run around and he is on record stating that as far as he was concerned, Paula Vennells lied to him. Not only to him but to the Select committee and to Parliament. He really is a remarkable person and loved by all the postmasters. We all owe him an enormous debt of gratitude. His appearances on television certainly helped restore my faith in humanity.

This entire problem was slowly achieving some publicity although nowhere near as much as it deserved given the stakes and situations postmasters had already endured. For me, I was just glad that things were getting somewhere. The pressure was mounting. This was never going to go away now.

The Post Office was running out of places to hide. A storm was slowly brewing.

11

The GLO and the Great Rock and Roll Swindle.

It's 7th Nov 2018 and the Group Litigation Order was finally launched at the Royal Courts of Justice in central London. This was going to be a series of trials, focussed mainly on the contractual arrangement between the Post Office and the postmasters, the Horizon System itself and 6 individual cases.

Behind closed doors, the presiding judge, Judge Fraser, had already ruled on 2 issues. The first was around the Post Office applying to change the timetable to fit in around their availability. Fraser threw that one out. The second judgment ruled on the Post Office's application to strike out almost three quarters of the lead claimant's evidence. Justice Fraser said: "The application by the defendant to strike out this evidence appears to be an attempt to keep evidence with which the defendant does not agree from being aired at all".

The judge then commented that any adverse publicity for the Post Office was not a matter of concern for the court if the evidence was relevant and admissible. He also warned against the aggressive conduct of this litigation, particularly in a group action of this nature. The application was dismissed. The Post Office are on the back foot already having seen the first 2 decisions go against them.

I attended the opening day in London. The court room was full. Both legal teams were in place, and both had wheeled in their own sack truck piled up with boxes of documents. To me, it was riveting from the off. The claimants were represented by Patrick Green QC and the Post Office by David Cavender QC. It was not quite what I was expecting. The presiding judge, Lord Justice Fraser, was younger and more "with it" than I had imagined, especially after the only other judge I had previously encountered, the one at my trial at Chester Crown Court, seemed a long way past retirement age. This gave me hope that he might truly understand the intricate technicalities of what was unfolding before him. He most certainly did.

This first of a series of public trials was named "The Common Issues Trial" primarily looking at the terms of the contract between the postmasters and the Post Office.

Once all the traditional introductory stuff was over, I

found the actual back and forth statements and legal arguments very interesting. Patrick Green QC was superb. A very clear and experienced orator. I began to feel slightly more confident that the truth would be exposed properly to Judge Fraser. I was surprised how little the judge interjected, he just sat there listening to the back-and-forth arguments, occasionally writing something down.

It was all new to me. A fascinating look into this legal world at the highest level. Amazingly the freelance journalist, Nick Wallis, was permitted to tweet out every word spoken during the trial. As far as I am aware this was uncommon and made a huge difference.

Next day I'm back at work and I have twitter live on my phone, following the trial through Nick Wallis' continuous live transcript and his own comments. As time went along this became a true courtroom drama. The watered down sporadic simplified updates from Our law firm just didn't work for me, not compared to hearing every word via Nick Wallis. My anxiety was sky high because I was all too aware that this was the only game in town and it had to work for us, this was it. It's taken years and years to get to this. What if we get steamrollered.

The Post Office's legal contentions were centred around

the following key arguments:

1. **Contractual relationship**

   - The Post Office argued that sub-postmasters were just independent businesspeople, agents, not employees, and operated under standard contracts that clearly defined their responsibilities. The contract was not relational, so they owed them no duty of care in any way. If anything went wrong, they were not obliged to do anything to assist.

   - It claimed that postmasters had full responsibility for their branch accounts and were liable for any shortfalls.

2. **Horizon IT system's reliability**

   - The Post Office contended that its Horizon IT system was robust and reliable.

   - It argued that any discrepancies within sub-postmasters' accounts were due to their own errors or dishonesty, rather than faults in the system.

3. **Right to suspend and terminate contracts**

- The Post Office maintained that it had the contractual right to suspend or terminate sub-postmasters without notice, particularly in cases where it believed there had been financial discrepancies or misconduct.

- It justified its use of criminal and civil actions against postmasters based on the belief that they were responsible for any missing funds.

4. **Discrepancies were the sole responsibility of Postmasters**

- The Post Office insisted that sub-postmasters had an obligation to balance their accounts daily and were solely accountable for any shortfalls.

- It argued that if postmasters signed off their accounts as correct, they could not later dispute the figures.

5. **Existence of a fair contractual process**

- The Post Office claimed that its contractual and

investigatory processes were fair and transparent.

- It defended the lack of disclosure regarding known Horizon errors, arguing that this information was not relevant to individual cases.

This was my first official insight in what the Post Office truly thought of us. Despite my investment of £154k and putting my house on the line, I was simply viewed as collateral damage.

The legal procedure did become difficult to follow at times, as things got bogged down in legal technicalities that were, on regular occasions, tricky to understand. But I followed intently all the same.

The common issue trial came to its conclusion and subsequently there was a long wait to hear how Judge Fraser was going to rule. Not being a lawyer, I wasn't sure whether the Post Office had scored points that were going to undermine the claimants or not. It did feel like our QC, Patrick Green, had done extremely well putting the realities of how the Post Office were treating postmasters in sharp focus. But would the law and the judge agree.

Judge Mr. Justice Fraser ultimately rejected the Post

Office's arguments, ruling on 15th March 2019 that:

The contracts were unfairly one-sided and **were** in fact relational.

He ruled that the Post Office exercised excessive control over postmasters.

Horizon did contain bugs and defects that could cause unexplained shortfalls.

The Post Office had mistreated postmasters and wrongfully pursued legal actions against them.

The handing down of Fraser's judgement proved to be a resounding win for the claimants. His harsh conclusions ruled that the Sub-postmaster's contract was indeed 'relational', meaning the Post Office **did** have a duty of care and could not treat postmasters in the manner they always had. Many other parts of the contract were ruled onerous and unenforceable. For instance, we were suspended without pay; this was ruled as wrong in law.

This was a huge win for us, and we now know it caused panic at the Post Office. Of course they tried to appeal this judgement, were refused, but appealed anyway. The appeal courts threw it out. The costs were awarded to our side and in the millions already. I was starting to believe we were going to be successful and win the overall litigation. You can never be sure at this level that the current law, as written, will *really* protect you from this kind of treatment, especially from a public company, but this was going well for us.

I was already aware that at the high end of litigation, it's not about justice, it's only about the minutiae of words and how they can be interpreted by either side. Quite a lot of law seems a very long time out of date and could go against you in a modern setting. But things are finally going our way. The Post Office are not in charge anymore. Or so it seemed.

The next trial was going to cover The Horizon System and any faults that may have caused the issues that sub-postmasters believed it had. My anxiety levels were way up and down, and at this time as I was really going through the mental mill. For so many times, I had thought we were getting somewhere only for the Post Office to pull the rug out from under us. Closing Second Sights' investigation, then refusing any mediation with me for example.

I am taking anti-anxiety tablets, but I'm still riddled with it.

I feel constantly on high alert that despite the litigation going our way, the Post Office would still do something to wreck everything.

My partner Donna and I spent almost every waking hour discussing every possible aspect of all this. It totally dominated our lives together. We are both pretty positive people and tried our best to keep our pecker up through it all, but honestly this was very draining. Years and years of it.

The Horizon trial

It's now March 2019 and the Horizon issues trial is underway. This trial is to focus on the Horizon system itself and whether its bugs, errors and defects had caused the discrepancies the 555 claimants said it had.

Once again, I'm at work and trying to keep abreast of it by reading Nick Wallis' tweets on a live thread. It's extremely detailed and at times difficult to understand all the technicalities of the software code and its possible faults. As the days went on it started to become clear that there were a lot more faults than had been originally exposed by Second Sights' unfinished investigation. The Post Office were coming up with bizarre arguments about the mere mathematical probability of any these faults affecting postmasters branch accounts. It was utterly nonsensical gobbledegook and Judge Fraser was on to it.

The following are the flawed arguments put forward by the Post Office and what the court found.

Post Office's arguments:

1. The Post Office claimed that its Horizon IT system was fundamentally reliable and that any discrepancies in sub-postmasters' accounts were due to user errors or dishonesty.

The court found that Horizon contained numerous bugs, errors and defects that did cause unexplained shortfalls. The system was not robust, and errors did occur without the knowledge of sub-postmasters.

2. The Post Office insisted that sub-postmasters had absolute responsibility for balancing their accounts and that they were always at fault for any shortfalls.

The court found that Horizon's errors did cause shortfalls without any mistake by postmasters. The Post Office had failed to properly investigate discrepancies and instead demanded immediate repayment from sub-postmasters.

3. The Post Office maintained that there was no evidence of widespread, systemic failures in Horizon and that any errors were isolated incidents.

The court found expert evidence showed that Horizon had multiple serious flaws affecting many branches and known issues were not properly disclosed to sub-postmasters or the courts in earlier prosecutions.

4. The Post Office claimed that it had no obligation to disclose known Horizon errors to sub-postmasters or in legal cases where postmasters were prosecuted.

The court ruled that the Post Office had acted oppressively by withholding crucial evidence. Internal documents showed that the Post Office was aware of Horizon errors but chose not to disclose them, even in criminal cases.

5. The Post Office asserted that it could not remotely alter branch accounts, implying that sub-postmasters were solely responsible for any discrepancies.

The court found that evidence revealed that Fujitsu

(Horizon's developer) did have remote access and did make changes to branch accounts.

This meant that financial records could be altered without sub-postmasters' knowledge.

6. Post Office asserted that the Courts should trust the Post Office's expert witnesses. The Post Office relied on expert witnesses to support its claims that Horizon was reliable.

Justice Fraser found that main Post Office's expert witness lacked independence and credibility. He wasn't qualified as an expert witness.

In contrast, the claimants' experts provided compelling evidence of systemic Horizon failures.

Chaos in the courtroom

So, the Post Office, obviously realising that they were going to lose this trial as well, decided to press the nuclear button and cause chaos in the courtroom. Only a couple of weeks into this trial and without warning, the Post Office tried to remove Judge Fraser. It's now become a board game. Snakes and ladders. All at great public expense.

I was watching Nick Wallis' twitter feed and he suddenly announced that a letter had been passed to Judge Fraser by the Post Office legal team. It was an application for him to recuse himself (stand down) on the grounds of apparent bias! the Post Office had enlisted Lord Grabiner QC, the most expensive QC in London to make this application. The trial was halted. I was on the verge of a panic attack. Lord Grabiner added that the application to recuse had "been looked at by another very senior person before the decision was taken".

The recusal application was opposed by the sub-postmasters' legal team and after a lengthy ruling, dismissed by the judge. This took many, many weeks.

This "other senior person" turned out to be Lord Neuberger, former head of the Supreme Court. The highest level it's possible to get. So, a labour Lord (Grabiner) and the former head of the Supreme Court were actively engaged in trying to derail the entire litigation for the postmasters who had a case, all for a very large personal fee. To me this is utterly reprehensible and without doubt immoral, but the legal system seems rife with both aspects.

Well I never! The costs for this recusal attempt were over £300k, of public money. It's obvious by now that these top end legal people will try anything and say anything, if the fee is right. No thoughts whatsoever for the postmasters who were positively winning the legal argument of course. That is not how the legal game works.

All this was an education into the absurdity of legal action at the highest level. The recusal attempt was dismissed and the Post Office appealed. Their appeal was thrown out on the grounds of it being absurd and without merit by appeal court Judge Coulson. A mind-boggling attempt to derail the entire case.

So, the top legal minds in the country came up with something absurd and without merit, at great public expense and trousered a huge amount of cash! To my mind it was a clear attempt to abuse the legal system to at least alter the course of justice. (A very difficult thing to prove of course). Absolutely disgraceful.

If Fraser had recused himself, that would have been it. No new judge, no restarted trial, nothing. We would have lost everything, and the Post Office knew it. That was the plan of course.

Signed Sealed Destroyed

We were dealing with an organisation willing to alter the course of justice on an industrial scale, protected by a legal system seemingly designed to serve the powerful. On a personal level, I was furious. Who do these fucking tosspots think they are?

When I found out that former Supreme Court head, Lord Neuberger, was involved I tracked down an email address and contacted him. I wrote a scathing email to him asking him what the hell did he think he was doing and that his actions were designed to fuck over hundreds of innocent postmasters. I got a response from his sister who told me she had passed it on to Neuberger. Incredibly, he replied.

He responded by saying that he "only advised on a narrow point of law" and that he had spent his career in human rights and being very mindful of miscarriages of justice. Translation, "I got my fee, its nothing personal."

Well, you are only as good as your last case; he will be forever remembered for this squalid episode. Ditto with Lord Grabiner. Apparently greedy, morally suspect people right at the very top. A Labour Lord too... wow, who knew.

It quickly became apparent to me, that the legal system is

stuffed to the gills with this sort. It has parallels with the music industry, there is so much money involved, it attracts the untrustworthy sharks, of course it does. It's all based on what individuals can personally gain from it, although this is not readily apparent when you see them in their fine suits and hear their plummy well-spoken voices, but during the later public inquiry, this was laid bare for all to see.

Thankfully, Judge Fraser did not recuse himself and released an 80-page ruling. Post Office appealed this too, the Court of Appeal backed him entirely, ruling the application was without merit and was an attempt to derail the entire litigation. After a delay of three weeks, the trial resumed. More and more details were uncovered showing the egregious way that the Post Office ignored correct procedures and conducted themselves in any way they saw fit. The fact they are funded by public money with a bottomless pocket meant they just rode roughshod over the usual expected procedures and made it up as they went along, always protected by the State. Incredible.

It's now December 2019 and we are all waiting on the hand down of Fraser's judgement.

Surprise settlement

I am at work, and I go to the toilet. I check twitter and to my astonishment I read that "The Post Office settles the GLO with a £57 million compensation payment" on the BBC's news feed. I am completely floored. I blinked at my phone screen, my heart pounding. Fifty-seven million? I read it again. That couldn't be right. We'd been fighting for years, had endured humiliation, poverty, and stress beyond belief, I felt like I'd been punched in the gut.

There was no warning that this was even on the cards. There had been no mention of any "mediation" going on at all. In fact, costs hearings with Judge Fraser were taking place for the next trial. What the hell was going on.

I immediately thought £57 million was really low considering there were 555 claimants. An average of just over £100K each, people had all sorts of different circumstances and claims, but this sum wasn't going to touch the sides. People had lost everything, their homes, their businesses, everything.

I thought hang on; the claimants were heading for a big win in the Horizon trial why stop now? It will never be in a better position. This seemed insane. On reading what the legal eagles were saying through the Law Gazette they were astonished too, the general feeling was that compensation would be in the hundreds of millions. Worst was to come, much worse. There was talk that the legal costs were to be deducted from the 57 million. Nothing is being confirmed by our law firm. They have gone very quiet. Very quiet indeed.

I took time off from work with stress because of this.

I travel to London with my partner and brother for the official hand down of Judge Fraser's final judgement on the Horizon issues. The big one. The one we have waited all these years for, in varying states of distress. Our law firm had advance copy of this but not us, the wronged.

Before the actual handing down, I arranged a meeting with a senior lawyer from our law firm to ask some burning questions. He told me to my face that this was the best outcome we could have got, considering the contents of the judgement. So of course, I thought we must not have won as comprehensively as was expected, we must have lost enough of the issues to impact the compensation level that much.

I then ask him how the mediation was so quick considering there are 555 claimants. He tells me that "mediation of this complexity takes a day". In my humble opinion, this was simply a downright bluff. (The mediation actually took 10 days). I'm not stupid and my brother Steve is quite knowledgeable around the subject of mediation, we both felt immediately he was not being straight with us. They have a duty to act in our best interests. In my opinion, something stinks already, something really stinks.

We go into the courtroom and Judge Fraser hands down the 313-page document with a bit of a speech about it. I am in a state of turmoil and the only thing I can remember him saying, was something about malicious prosecution being a legal route and he was going to rule that as a part of the judgement and the judgement is now in the public domain.

Some key findings in Mr. Justice Fraser's final ruling:

1. Horizon was not robust or reliable

Fraser found that Horizon contained numerous bugs, errors and defects that did cause discrepancies in sub-postmasters' accounts.

The system was not remotely robust, despite the Post Office's repeated claims to the contrary.

2. Horizon bugs did cause unexplained shortfalls

The court ruled that bugs in Horizon did generate false shortfalls, meaning sub-postmasters could not be held liable for financial discrepancies they did not cause.

3. The Post Office's conduct was "Institutional obstinacy"

Justice Fraser condemned the Post Office's aggressive and unreasonable behaviour, stating that it had shown "institutional obstinacy" in refusing to acknowledge faults in Horizon.

4. The Post Office had misled courts in criminal cases

Fraser found that the Horizon system contained flawed data and was not remotely reliable.

He ruled that it had withheld key evidence about Horizon errors, misleading both sub-postmasters and the courts.

5. Remote access was possible – and undisclosed

Contrary to the Post Office's claims, Fraser ruled that Fujitsu (Horizon's developer) had remote access to branch accounts and could alter transaction data without sub-postmasters' knowledge.

This finding was crucial because it undermined the Post Office's repeated assertions that only sub-postmasters were responsible for their accounts.

Final Judgment Summary:

Mr. Justice Fraser's ruling was so devastating for the Post Office. He concluded that:

Horizon was fundamentally flawed.

The Post Office's behaviour was oppressive. sub-postmasters had been wrongly blamed and prosecuted.

Victory

It is a comprehensive victory for the claimants. He ruled that the Horizon system wasn't remotely reliable and **had** caused the types of discrepancies the postmasters claimed it had. He ruled that various witnesses from the Post Office and Fujitsu had sought to mislead him. He ruled that the Post Office arguments were akin to the "Earth being flat". A total success for the claimants.

What on earth was our senior lawyer talking about when he said, "This was the best outcome we could have got, taking into account the contents of the judgement"? Of course this was now confirmed as utter nonsense. How and why had this happened?

All the claimants in attendance for the handing down were taken into a room with our senior lawyer and Patrick Green QC. Patrick Green was musing at how well the case had gone and what a success the settlement had been. There were glum faces all around the room. Our senior lawyer then explained that after the fees to the funder and to our law firm, there was roughly 9 to 11 million left for the claimants.

There was a collective groan, personally I was in shock. Our senior lawyer immediately went on the defensive. "Hang on, hang on, you would have never even got this off the ground without us. No other law firm was prepared to take this on apart from us". This cut no ice with anybody in the room, no ice at all.

There was no doubt that our law firm had put in a tremendous amount of work, they really had been amazing. How they pieced all this together into an actual legal challenge, sifting through so much information over so many years affecting hundreds of people, beggars' belief. They had faced off and been successful against a nasty untrustworthy Post Office, brilliantly presented throughout by Patrick Green QC. A superb legal job in all aspects.

But the outcome was a disaster for the claimants. The settlement agreed was not going to go anywhere near addressing our claims.

We were all very well aware that there would be large deductions for the fees, remember the earlier document about levels of compensation and possible costs? But it was a common feeling amongst us and other legal eagles that compensation would be in the 100's of millions. Even with a hefty fee for the legal work and funders there would still be enough to at least approach our losses. So this can't be real can it? This cannot be it.

As we now know the true cost of the compensation required is now over £1.5 Billion! £57 million **was** utterly useless. Absolutely hopeless. Who on god's earth had agreed this on our behalf?

We all came out of the meeting utterly shocked. I had a few tears while wandering aimlessly around the area outside the courtroom. I couldn't quite take it in. Despite all the years, all the disappointments, all the travelling to meetings, the years of talking and talking with my partner about very little else. The effort of dealing with 3 different law firms, starting from the beginning every time, extended periods of waiting for any news, the constant unrelenting anxiety in my body, the bouts of depression, the pressure of knowing it could all go wrong, It's difficult to truly describe the impact this situation had on me and the people around me for many, many years. Yet here we are, an amazing and resounding victory in the litigation, then it all secretly ends, abruptly, with compensation that only seems to work for the funders and our law firm. Almost all claimants will still be in deep debt.

For the ones who did not receive a criminal conviction this was the end of the road. It had been written into the settlement agreement that no further legal action is allowed. Most of the sub-postmasters had lost everything and were financially ruined. Those without a conviction seemed to have been royally shafted. Wow, how terribly trusting and naive we had all been. Something is wrong.

Our law firm immediately began monitoring Facebook and Twitter. They knew there would be a backlash from this. I received an email from them telling me, "Not to say anything bad about the Post Office as it could affect your compensation". Excuse me? How dare they say such a thing? This stink is growing. What on earth is going on.

I do go on to say something disparaging on Twitter about the sudden end to the litigation and get a phone call from a key member of the "Steering committee". This committee was set up to do the negotiating and agreeing of things on our behalf, so that our law firm didn't have to communicate every little detail to all 555 claimants every time. she tells me "Our law firm are not happy". I said ***I'm*** not happy, ***they*** should be ecstatic. I'm to get very little and have to start again while the company partners will be handsomely remunerated.

I told her I will need to speak to her again once I've read the finer details of this dreadful settlement agreement.

The shutters were now firmly down. Our law firm were far more interested in what people were saying on social media than communicating with the postmasters. I thought at the time that this might not end too well for them. The truth will out. When this was finally surfaced it may reveal another scandal. This is how I felt.

Unfortunately, in my opinion, they presumed we were all a bit stupid, a bit thick not versed in legal realities and that we "wouldn't understand". But I believed they had made a grave error with that presumption.

The great Morrissey once mused, "There's always someone somewhere, with a big nose who knows, who'll trip you up and laugh when you fall". The truth will out. I have been working with a legal costs lawyer who is determined to get to the bottom of this. I have absolutely no interest whatsoever with who it might upset. That ship sailed many, many moons ago. I want the truth, and many others do too. They cannot get away without a full explanation. It will be exposed, and I am determined it will be. If I am wrong in my assumptions that this agreement was not in our best interests, then so be it. No problem. But if I'm not?… well.

I could be wrong, but I do not like the way I was treated.

12

The Settlement agreement.

This was the document agreed on my behalf without consultation, without warning, and for me personally, without a credible explanation. It was signed off ensuring most claimants were shackled with meagre compensation, permanently barred from seeking further recourse and, crucially, without Post Office Ltd admitting liability. That last bit really sticks in my craw.

It was, in my opinion, the most outrageous conclusion imaginable given the overwhelming success in the litigation. The claimants were in a **strong legal position**, yet the agreement handed the advantage straight back to the Post Office. The only lifeline for me was that Judge Fraser had ruled that malicious prosecution was still an option for convicted claimants. Without that, I suspect the Post Office would have ensured we had absolutely no remaining legal avenues.

For all the other claimants without convictions, this was the end.

Absolutely amazing, don't you think? For the claimants without convictions, this was the end of the road. These were people who had lost everything. Businesses, homes, savings, and even family relationships. And this was their final offer? In my opinion, the sheer lack of common sense, fairness, and basic decency in this agreement is staggering.

It eventually transpires that 'mediation' took place between "The steering committee" and the Post Office lawyers. One main member of this committee did not attend every meeting in person. Given the total lack of transparency, it is my strong opinion that the non-lawyers were possibly steamrollered into agreeing this tragic and disastrous settlement. It's hard to blame the steering committee for this. I'm almost certain they were being convinced that they had no other option, so, who was to blame? Perhaps the government told Post Office that this was as far as they could go, we don't know. We still don't know.

I clearly cannot know for sure if that is true, but I struggle to see how anyone, unless completely outmanoeuvred or misled, would agree to this deal. We had just won a major legal battle, exposing the Post Office's conduct as oppressive and dishonest, about to go to the next very important trial, and yet we were to settle for a sum that didn't even remotely address our claims. Even experienced legal commentators at the Law Gazette were baffled by the settlement's low figure and terrible timing. How was the amount **£57.5 million** decided? Who exactly determined this figure?

How was this related to our actual claims? It wasn't. So as anybody with any braincells would.... I smell a rat.

Get this, written into the settlement, convicted postmasters were settled to zero. £0. The agreement actually *stipulated* that we were to get nothing. I realised immediately that the Post Office lawyers had drafted this entire agreement. Some wording stated that if the steering committee decided to give us some of the compensation, the Post Office have no power to stop them. Wow, how generous. You really secured a great deal with that.

How can any of this be possibly in my, or any other claimants', best interests. It wasn't. It felt like it was in the Post Office, the funders and our law firm's interests. But not the sub-postmasters. The work's cat could see that.

What has happened to the document showing possible compensation levels I showed you earlier? Remember it stated that if the compensation total reached 47 million an individual with a claim for £1 million could expect around £729,730. The compensation paid by the Post Office was in fact **£57 million**, but my claim would be valued at £0. I did realise that these original figures were "subject to change" but hey hang on a minute this is absolutely astounding. That important document seemed to be nothing but figures scrawled on the back of a fag packet.

Never mind anxiety, I am panicking now. Convicted claimants have to start again from the very beginning and sue the bloody Post Office, as individuals, for malicious prosecution with no further help from our law firm. A very, very difficult bar to reach in law and, in fact, rarely reached.

London legal advisors Kingsley Napley, in an article on their website, state that "malicious prosecution claims are rarely successful due to the tall hurdle of proving that the proceedings were maliciously brought without reasonable and probable cause". All this is apparently in my best interests. Like I said, the fact that this route is even in there is down to Judge Fraser including it in the hand down of his judgment. If he hadn't, I am of the strong opinion that this would have been signed away too. The Post Office would have certainly wanted that.

So, standing back a second, just to re-cap, the convictions of the sub-postmasters, were the **only reason** there was something to litigate. The whole premise of why law firms and funders took this on in the first instance, the whole grounds of this legal action. Yet we were settled to zero, having to start again, saddled with years of further legal action, but on our own.

Why no help? Because included in the agreement was an actual clause stipulating that our law firm could not assist the claimants in any way for any reason, going forward. This is absolutely set in stone that they are bailing out at this juncture, tough shit, you are cast out and on your own now. This was stunning to say the least, and for me, the last straw.

I'm sorry, but in my opinion, this felt like a betrayal. It certainly appeared that commercial interest had taken priority over justice, whilst leaving us in the lurch. Maybe this was standard procedure, but to me it smacked of greed. It felt immoral. It presumably is the way it is, and any law firm would have behaved in the same way, but I found this behaviour deeply disturbing. I was never, ever going to forget this. Dragged over the coals once again. Cheers guys. You do realise our lives are fucked up don't you? business is business I suppose. Jesus wept.

Some law firms are awarded "Lexcel accreditation". supposedly top draw brownie points for client relations. Keeping clients properly updated with clarity of fee levels and costs information. As far as I'm concerned, this did not happen. We were all completely in the dark regarding the circumstances surrounding mediation and the money. In my experience, the accreditation didn't reflect how we were actually treated. I'm sure this stuff is all standard practice but from my position, it really felt diabolical.

Of course, I complained bitterly in a long email to them, their reply had some scant details but basically said that they only had to deal with the steering committee and not us as individuals. Whilst technically correct, it's very poor given these extraordinary circumstances. They could use that as a shield from the backlash.

They actually said that if they hadn't given us some cash out of the goodness of their heart, the funding agreement as stated, meant they would have been entitled to take every single penny of the £57 million. So we should be grateful that they are not going to take all their fees. WTF. Did they really think this wasn't going to be looked at ?…. well, I can assure you in the future it's going to be looked at in immense detail, this is not going to go away.

Signed Sealed Destroyed

I telephoned the member of the steering committee, (she had done a hell of a lot of great work for us, spanning years) and I told her that after reading the settlement agreement fully, I'm very unhappy. She actually said, "what part of the settlement agreement are you not happy with"!! I said ALL OF IT, but particularly the fact I have been settled to zero, the Post Office are not admitting liability and I have to go it alone and start again with malicious prosecution action. Explain to me the bits that are positive for us.

She blathers on about how the Post Office were only offering around 2 million and to get 57 million was a fantastic result. I'm not having it and told her this was an absolute disaster for all of us, and she ends up in tears. Something is very wrong. Very, very wrong. We have never found out the truth about all this, but I will get to the bottom of it somehow.

Jesus Christ, I'm crestfallen, Donna is crestfallen. What shall we do tomorrow? All the effort to get to the GLO, all the time taken out of my life to get to the GLO and it's imploded into a mess. There are plenty of affected postmasters who are really pissed off with this. It's agonising, we are getting older and older.

Signed Sealed Destroyed

I took it upon myself to have the settlement agreement analysed independently. I didn't want to just carry on going apeshit about it from a personal emotional angle only, after all, maybe I was completely wrong here. Maybe I was over-reacting. I was suffering from severe anxiety, after all.

The following is what this separate analysis concluded.

'The Group Litigation Order (GLO) settlement agreement in the Post Office Horizon IT scandal is widely criticised for not adequately compensating the 555 postmasters involved. Although the group secured a £57.75 million settlement after their legal action revealed systemic failures in the Horizon IT system, the net compensation available to the postmasters was significantly reduced. Legal fees consumed approximately £46 million of the settlement, leaving only about £11.5 million for distribution among the claimants. This translated to relatively small payouts for individuals, particularly when compared to the life-altering consequences many endured, such as financial ruin, reputational damage, and wrongful convictions.

The settlement agreement also had provisions that limited the postmasters' ability to pursue further compensation. As part of the agreement, claimants relinquished their rights to future claims against the Post Office, which became a contentious point after the government announced broader compensation schemes for others affected by the scandal. This left the GLO claimants, paradoxically, as some of the least compensated individuals among the victims of the Horizon IT debacle.

Critics argue that the settlement primarily benefited the Post Office and the legal system not the claimants. The process prioritised a resolution that protected the Post Office from further liability, while the legal fees highlighted the cost of fighting for justice in such cases, all at the claimants' expense.

Convicted claimants, such as yourself, faced a particularly harsh outcome in the Post Office Horizon GLO settlement. Despite being among the most severely affected—many wrongfully convicted, financially ruined, and personally devastated—the compensation process failed to account for your unique circumstances. The settlement effectively wiped out any meaningful restitution for convicted claimants, primarily because of how legal and administrative costs consumed the settlement fund.'

So I was right. After years of stress and hope, I felt we were betrayed at the very end. This felt like legal nonsense dressed up as justice. Abysmal.

Incredibly, this whole subject was not explored during the entire 3-year public inquiry! Many postmasters I have spoken to are dismayed about this. It just doesn't make sense. How can such a huge trial and its contentious outcome not be looked at properly? Considering the inquiry has delved deeply into virtually every little aspect of the scandal, it's another complete mystery.

13

The Empty Promise of Justice

When the Group Litigation Order (GLO) settlement was finalised, the law firm representing the 555 claimants justified settling convicted postmasters to zero on the basis that this would enable us to pursue claims for malicious prosecution against the Post Office. This explanation might seem logical on the surface, but in my reality, it only compounded the injustice we had already endured

The law firm claimed that by settling convicted claimants at zero, we could still pursue malicious prosecution cases against the Post Office. But I felt that this was a sleight of hand.

Malicious prosecution is one of the hardest cases to prove. It requires evidence that the prosecution not only lacked reasonable and probable cause but was driven by malice, an extraordinarily high legal bar.

Most claimants, after years of financial ruin and emotional exhaustion, could not afford another gruelling court battle.

The law firm knew all of this. Yet they presented it as a fair trade-off when to my mind, it simply locked us out of meaningful compensation.

I did eventually receive some hand-out money from the GLO settlement. I truly believe that the sum I received was because I shouted up against all this and I was a vocal annoyance. The loudest voices got something. The quiet ones got less. I could be wrong of course. But in life this seems one of its unspoken rules.

Others also received small amounts from the 11.5 million. But these amounts did not address our claims in any way. For me personally, less than 3%.

The settlement agreement created a glaring disparity. Those who were wrongfully prosecuted suffered the most severe consequences; criminal records, imprisonment and financial devastation, yet received almost nothing. Meanwhile, others in the GLO who experienced financial losses but were not prosecuted, at least received some compensation (albeit woeful after deductions for legal costs) but were legally barred from any further claims. I felt this outcome was indefensible.

To add insult to injury, all claimants in the GLO were

barred from accessing subsequent compensation schemes, such as the Historical Shortfall Scheme (HSS). These schemes, set up to provide meaningful restitution to victims of the Horizon scandal, excluded GLO participants entirely. This left many trapped in legal limbo, unable to pursue further claims. Catastrophic for many claimants as they were now in a legal cul-de-sac, despite losing everything.

Incredibly, those who never took legal action ended up in a better position than those who fought for justice. Our law firm's stance regarding potential malicious prosecution raised serious questions to me, about the adequacy of our representation.

In the end, who was truly helped? Settling convicted claimants to zero seems to have benefited the Post Office more than the victims. By ensuring that we couldn't claim compensation within the settlement, the Post Office avoided paying the full extent of damages owed.

The Lasting Impact

For convicted claimants like me the settlement was clearly not a resolution. We were failed by the Post Office, failed by the legal system and, to me, by those who were supposed to represent our interests. The promise of suing for malicious prosecution rang hollow when the resources, time, and emotional toll of such a battle felt beyond reach.

Any action is now going to take many more years without any guarantee of success. My partner along with myself felt utterly devastated. I had long been suffering with mental fatigue and now this was clearly going to be severely compounded. The years were passing by and we both so desperately wanted to get this whole situation out of our lives. We thought we were on the verge of that happening. We talked about perhaps it was **never** going to end in our favour. Maybe it was all just a pipe dream, and the legal system and corporate organisations cannot be beaten in the end.

We did win the case after all but even that didn't seem to mean anything.

14

Big Money always seems to sour things.

I am then informed that our law firm are withholding funds to cover possible further liabilities, I thought maybe from *us*, the "client".

I felt we were now being treated a bit like cattle and just a nuisance now they had banked their fees. We were now surplus to requirements.

Remember, our law firm were now legally barred from representing any postmaster for any reason going forward? Well, later in this saga and after a hell of a lot of pressure, the Government decided that the settlement agreement **was** in fact unfair to the GLO postmasters and were prepared to top up the meagre amount people received from it.

Have a guess who was back in the frame? Yes, our law firm. The same firm that had waved us all goodbye immediately the settlement was agreed. Hmmm

Given they signed a legally binding undertaking to have absolutely no further involvement, signed on behalf of all affected postmasters, how is this structured?

The moment more Government money was available to them, the clauses in the agreement went straight out of the window. Not legally binding after all, all set aside for convenience's sake, I'm sure there is a legal phrase that covers all this stuff.

There was no wrongdoing, but I personally found all this to be rather bizarre, so, with plenty of time on my hands, I started to research heavily into the subject of Law Firms and how the business model operates.

To be honest, I wish I had gone to university as a mature student and studied law. I have had the time! I would have been much more informed of course and not had to rely on others so much. I regret this now.

Oh dear, what do I discover.

So, where do I start? Obviously not all, but it is well documented in research papers I have read by legal research company Lexology, that a percentage of these organisations engage in dubious practices as their modus operandi. I do not aim these practices at **any law firm** whatsoever, I'm only relating what I have read, but the glossy brochures law firms hand out seem to be very different to the reality of what is going to happen to you, the "client".

Even calling customers "clients" in my opinion is a subtle way of seducing you into believing you are engaging ultra-professional, highly intelligent and ethical people to help.

The following paragraphs contain some hard to swallow truths. How any of this relates to the money made from all legal work conducted by various firms from all sides related to the post office scandal I will never know, perhaps not at all, from my own experience we were never billed as clients because the bills were simply paid from the compensation claimed.

However, my research has revealed that certain practices some law firms operate are accepted as totally normal. I was quite astonished with some of the details.

It is no secret that legal work is expensive, but what shocked me was just how much of it is designed to **inflate costs** rather than deliver justice. The practices below are widely documented in legal research and explain why legal cases seem to drag on endlessly.

6-minute billing. As the "client" it's totally normal that you will be billed for every 6 minutes of work done on your behalf. If you have a 3-minute phone call with them, of course this is rounded up to 6 for billing purposes.

Despite enormous advances in information technology, current legal work takes as long now as it did in the days of parchment and quill letter writing. Now I know why. It is of zero interest to a law firm for things to be quicker. The hourly rates are into the many hundreds of pounds and, for some so called "Magic Circle" firms, it's in the thousands.

Of course they are not going to be swift. It simply does not make business sense, does it?

Invoice padding. For some law firms, various erroneous things are added to the bill to bump up the invoice significantly. Phantom hours, fictitious time sheets, charging for "research" when it's their normal area of expertise and double billing (charging two clients for a single piece of work).

If they decide to work through their lunchtime, you can get

charged for the lunch. They even bill for the storage of client documents, I never imagined that this was even a thing, but yes.... clients pay for this storage. It must be really top drawer organised personal storage!

All this appears to be normal practise. Some of it is, of course, a fraudulent practise. Ironically, it is theft, a criminal offence. Oh the irony.

A lawyer personally known to me, told me, "The billing is purely for time spent, not the quality of the work done". This is all akin to dodgy car repairers inventing work they haven't actually done, since the client has no clue.

Legal research undertaken in 2024 by Lexology, notes, "some lawyers believe that time padding is almost endemic, with practices such as rounding up time, billing for multitasked activities, and retroactively adjusting hours being common." Lexology note that 35.9% of legal firms **admitted** adding time that "hadn't been incurred".

So we can see that the law firm exists only to max out the costs to the "client". This could be said of all businesses of course, but the client is so completely in the dark about how law firms operate compared to other mainstream businesses they are effectively "lambs to the slaughter".

All at the expense of the poor hapless "client", many of whom are desperately needing help. Utterly atrocious in my opinion. If we are talking morals here.

It's obvious this needs serious reform. Unfortunately, the SRA, or Solicitors Regulation Authority, the body that is supposed to police this kind of activity, has been exposed to be wanting in this and many other areas. Despite mounting evidence of legal and ethical breaches by solicitors instructed by the Post Office, the SRA has appeared slow, or entirely absent in launching investigations. It has seemed hesitant to exercise its powers against lawyers from high profile firms despite the draconian powers they can use. For victims, campaigners and observers, the SRA's inaction further undermines trust in regulatory oversight.

Some lawyers may believe they are untouchable, but their industry is not immune to disruption. Just as the music industry collapsed when Napster and streaming services made CD sales obsolete, AI will eventually dismantle large parts of the legal profession.

Once people realise, they can get accurate legal advice from AI **for free**, rather than pay a lawyer £500 an hour to tell them something generic, the legal industry will be in serious trouble. And you know what? for some firms, **Good**. The chickens are coming home to roost.

Of course, not all firms are like this, it's a minority, but the bad eggs can tend to bring the thing into disrepute. Knowing this kind of activity went on just compounded the anxiety I was already suffering every single day. Of course, there is absolutely no empathy for anything like that.

Maybe sometimes it's better to stay in the dark. Not knowing things can be bliss!

15

Convictions are overturned.

On the 23rd April 2021, I travelled to the Royal Courts of Justice in London where I and 38 other convicted sub-postmasters had our criminal convictions officially overturned. When I arrived outside the historic building there were a lot of TV vans and press photographers milling around. I bumped into journalist Nick Wallis and we had a cheerful chat as some of the main legal QC's were arriving and filing in through the grand entrance. This was before Covid restrictions had ceased so plenty of people were wearing masks and socially distancing.

I went in and was directed to one of the many courthouses in use in this grand building. In Courtroom 5, I was given a seat, distanced from the only two other postmasters allowed in the same room due to the Covid restrictions. It was all quite surreal looking back.

There was an announcement on a Tannoy installed in this room, regarding the circumstances and our reason for gathering there on this day. Then, the names of those deemed wrongfully convicted were read aloud, one by one.

Signed Sealed Destroyed

This took quite a while and around 30 names had been read out, but I hadn't heard my name yet! I was getting increasingly anxious, I thought what if I'm **not** going to have my conviction overturned. Maybe I am one who the Post Office has scuppered etc. All irrational thoughts but it was very nerve-racking waiting to hear my name.

Then, at last, I heard it. "Scott Darlington, conviction overturned on both counts." My breath caught. The words rang in my ears. I dropped my head into my hands, overcome with sheer relief. It was over. I was no longer a criminal.. Jesus Christ it's really happened. I'm not a criminal anymore, its gone.

The Court of Appeal did not just overturn our convictions, it went further, declaring that the prosecutions themselves were an "affront to justice". This was an extraordinary ruling, something almost unheard of in British legal history

This is an excerpt from the official judgement.

In a historic decision handed down this morning, the Court of Appeal held that the prosecution of sub-postmasters by Post Office Limited between 2003 and 2013 was an abuse of process and an "affront to justice".

An affront to justice. Wow that phrase hit me hard. This wasn't just a courtroom win; this was an admission that what had happened to us was completely indefensible.

The Court of Appeal has found that the investigative and disclosure failings of Post Office Limited were "so egregious as to make the prosecution of any of the Horizon cases an affront to the conscience of the court" and that, in their conduct of the prosecutions, the Post Office "reversed the burden of proof".

Reversed the burden of proof. That was the most damning part. It meant that the Post Office had forced innocent people, hardworking sub-postmasters, to prove their innocence, rather than the other way around. It's a cornerstone of British justice that someone is innocent until proven guilty. The Post Office had torn that apart.

It is extremely rare for the Court of Appeal to decide that a prosecution has amounted to an affront to justice. That such a finding has been made in relation to so many cases, and in relation to the conduct of a single private prosecutor, is unprecedented.

We had spent years trying to convince people that we had been wronged. We had been ignored, belittled, called liars.

Yet now, here it was, written in black and white, we had been victims of the worst miscarriage of justice in British legal history.

My brother was waiting outside. We hugged and the atmosphere was all quite emotional really. We stayed around for a while in a state of euphoria while photos were taken and interviews given to the waiting press. We then decided we would try and get a drink somewhere.

Most places were closed due to the covid restrictions, but Steve knew of a wine bar near Embankment underground station that was open.

We flagged down a taxi and as we passed the crowds outside the Royal Courts we spot Ron Warmington from Second Sight, Lee Castleton OBE and his father, they jump in and off we go.

Sure enough the wine bar is open, subject to social distancing, and we get a table outside. We are joined by fellow sub-postmaster Chris Trousdale and Ron kindly gets a nice bottle of wine in to kick things off. What a great afternoon it was. The wine flowed and everybody was in high spirits. We clinked glasses, a toast to freedom, to justice and for the first time in years, laughter came easily.

We had been through hell, but today, we had won. All very surreal now but at the time it was very real.

It did cross my mind that surely the route to compensation would be swift after this ruling, I mean, it's in the bag now, isn't it?

I was very wrong, again!

16

Starting all over again.

Now I have to engage legal firm number 4, to take on the malicious prosecution action on my behalf. There are a few firms in the frame including Howe and Co, the firm I took my contract to in 2010. I choose Hudgells Solicitors. They had already taken on quite a few postmasters as "clients" and seemed to be a bit further down the line than the other law firms.

I had a zoom call with the boss, Neil Hudgell, and confirmed with him that they would be taking this on, and off we go again.

All the documents that I had in my possession from the time this disaster happened to me had been sent to the original law firm, Shoosmiths. These documents were then released to our previous law firm. I also took quite a pile of further documents to their offices in Manchester.

All this has now had to come to Hudgells, and they have identified that some things are missing. Hudgells are repeatedly having to ask me if I have various things that I have previously sent to our previous law firm!

They need to request our previous law firm again for various things, how can there be things missing? This document storage the clients are charged for doesn't seem too good after all does it. Is this simply a mistake? Or incompetence? Or more likely they couldn't give a hoot now they have finished dealing with us. Nothing ever seems to work properly, does it?

So, from the start this is going very, very slowly. The depression drags on, I'm getting older. Time is slipping away. I have so many things I want to do with my partner.

I want to get this thing out of my life, but it feels as far away as ever. Donna is also at the end of her tether.

She has had to suffer the same anxiety and constant disappointment as I have over all these years. She has been a constant support, and I guess we have supported each other through all this. Why she hasn't caved in I will never know. She has certainly had her moments, but she is a strong girl. She could have chosen not to stay in this relationship at the beginning because we met when this was just turning sour for me in 2008. She has been great. She has seen it through to this point with me all the way.

Signed Sealed Destroyed

The effect of this scandal hasn't just affected me, it has affected everybody around me. My partner, my ex, my daughter, my father and my brother.

My brother is completely tired of it, and he has backed off totally for his sanity. I don't blame him. His life is busy enough without this continuous drain on him.

I need to say something about Neil Hudgell. He has been incredibly good on both a professional and personal level. He always makes himself available for a chat, anytime. Considering how many his firm are representing and working for, this alone is remarkable.

He has had to put up with my belligerent attitude at times. When progress has been slow and I have moaned, he has constantly been in touch to reassure me that things are in fact moving forward. If I have disagreed with the way things work, he has calmly explained in easy-to-understand terms the reality of certain laws and circumstances.

How he remains a calm and seemingly relaxed guy I really don't know, he must have a hell of a lot of people texting and phoning him all the time! A true good guy.

It's now 2025. I was convicted in 2010.

My daughter Kitty was 8 years old when this situation began, she's 25 now and not only is it still not over, but it also still feels like there is a long way to go. She has known her dad has been in this trouble for most of her life. It really pains me to know that. Amazingly she seems unaffected by it all and very level headed but I know it has impacted her. How she would be as a person if this had never happened, I will never know. But it is something I think about.

It really pains me to realise how my situation has affected others.

17

The public inquiry.

As I write this book, the Public Inquiry has just concluded. It actually started in September 2020 as a non-statutory inquiry. The goal then was to provide some answers but no accountability.

Essentially a PR exercise allowing it to appear "cooperative" while dodging accountability. Only after multiple convictions were overturned on two counts and intense media scrutiny did the chair of the inquiry, Sir Wyn Williams, request it becoming a statutory inquiry. This meant for the first time witnesses could be legally compelled to give evidence, removing the ability for key Post Office executives and government officials to dodge responsibility.

This was good news for us and crucial because as a non-statutory inquiry, the miscreants who are responsible for this tragedy would have scuttled under a rock. Precisely what they were hoping for. I'm sure this was bad news for the top executives. They would be compelled to appear.

Along with many, many other victims of this scandal, I attended on 17th feb 2022 to give my own evidence during the first phase, known as The Human Impact phase. I wanted to be abrasive and cutting about everything I have encountered so far, but I kept a lid on it and calmly answered the questions posed by the council to the inquiry and said what I needed to say. Many others were far more scathing than I.

[Link to my video testimony](https://www.youtube.com/watch?v=JFRqmS2WuA0&t=20s)
https://www.youtube.com/watch?v=JFRqmS2WuA0&t=20s

Counsel to the Inquiry, the people tasked with unravelling the complex history of this scandal, specifically Jason Beer KC, have been absolutely incredible. Collating huge amounts of evidence to present in front of the chair of the inquiry. An incredible skill. All the KC's questioning of the never-ending list of people called to this inquiry showed they had incredible technical knowledge of the Horizon system and the legal ramifications of what happened. I take my hat off to these amazing people.

I, along with all the other affected sub-postmasters, wanted to see and hear from the type of people that ruined so many lives. What an awful type they turned out to be!

From the people that operate the helpline, the investigators, auditors, team leaders, lawyers and legal admin staff, executives, board members and every other role that makes up the structure of Post Office Ltd, so much incompetence, malpractice and deliberate efforts to skew the law has been revealed, it has been utterly shocking.

The Post Office's legal team **knowingly withheld exculpatory evidence (evidence that would have halted the GLO trial)**, misled the courts, and manipulated witness statements, actions that any reasonable person would consider **a conspiracy to pervert the course of justice.**

The fact that they systematically destroyed the lives of hundreds of innocent people, while ensuring no Post Office executive was ever brought to account, shows this was not mere incompetence, it was a calculated, criminal abuse of the justice system.

They took everybody they needed to along with them, almost all went willingly, using stooges to provide expert advice in criminal trials who were not even qualified to be even called experts. Twisting the wording of PR spin and speeches by the CEO and others senior executives resulting in blatant lies being told to Parliament and under oath at select committee hearings.

People were signing witness statement that they themselves had not written, the lawyers having written them on their behalf, itself a criminal offence. This is a common law offence of perverting the course of justice. If someone knowingly signs a false witness statement or allows one to be submitted in their name in criminal proceedings, they could be prosecuted for this offence. The legal firm that drafted the statement could also be prosecuted for the same offence. But will they?

The Post Office legal department constantly passed information to the board that the "system was fine" and not to blame. The board were so woeful, they did not bother or want to find out for themselves the truth and just hid behind these "assurances". What were they actually doing about this? Very little, it transpired.

All the layers of management, from the bottom to the very top, ignored all the obvious signs that things were drastically wrong. They only cared about their personal salary and kudos of the "role" they were playing. They most certainly did not want to open any can of worms even though many people had gone to prison. Totally unforgivable in any circumstances.

The hollow apologies that some of these witnesses proffered rang hollow to me, really hollow. There would have been none at all if they hadn't been compelled to appear. What a motley crew. In my opinion, most of them appeared to be fucking useless.

Donna and I were in attendance for the visit of Paula Vennells, all three days of her. The room was packed. This was the woman who, although she didn't start the scandal, presided over the cover up for many, many years. Incredibly, she had left the organisation in the middle of the GLO high court case, obviously realising the Post Office under her tenure was in very big trouble, with a payoff and an CBE!

She arrived at the inquiry with a security team of minders at a cost of £80,000 of public money. The Post Office has never given two hoots about misusing public money on a grand scale.

We wanted to see her squirm, having to answer uncomfortable questions under oath. She was in tears on several occasions when cornered by documents that revealed her actions. But the tears were for herself not for the many people she damaged. Awful woman. An ordained priest too. What can anybody say about that? She did not start this problem, but she spent the longest time covering it up. How does she sleep at night?

When bailed out of her position at the Post Office with a large golden handshake and a CBE, she managed to secure a top job at the NHS!

See how it all works at this level yet?

C-suite job titles

As I have previously said, this inquiry has revealed the type of people that populate corporate entities, law firms and the ancillary industries that feed off all this to be a different mindset than I could ever be, and to be honest, could ever believe existed.

The Post Office, for instance, is stuffed to the gills with nothing but "yes men". People who are infected with a type of indoctrination I have never encountered before.

The type that are fiercely proud to work for a brand, love the "colleague bonding" away-days, corporate hospitality, always happy to unquestionably follow the company line and repeat any company mantra they are required to, whether it's utter PR nonsense or not.

This type of person is clearly employed for a reason, they are unlikely to ever rock the boat and certainly hand-picked. They are also very keen on the names of their "roles" and boy, these names are mind-numbing. I am unsure why people find their titles so important. These same people were responsible for ruining so many lives.

Not all of these are Post Office roles but these are examples of the kind of job title folly perpetrated by corporate entities. How about Chief listening officer, Chief growth officer, Chief experience officer, Chief learning officer, even Chief happiness officer (I kid you not!)

I wanted to find out where and how these people get the so called top-end roles that ultimately damaged so many postmasters.

Having all the time in the world, I researched why there **are** so many C-suite job titles. I found an article written by Russel Fleischer, General partner with technology investment firm Battery Ventures. He remarks that *"Some companies like to craft new positions with fancy titles just to appear like they are paying attention to a particular business function. Others* *use C-level titles to combat the shortage of high-level talent in sought after fields. CEOs and recruiters' figure that if they give someone a "chief something" title instead of a more traditional role name, a candidate is more likely to sign on the dotted line."*

This is just as I suspected, to be honest.

To me, a lot of this is bordering on primary school mentality. Maybe they feel they need the badge and the faux superiority. It's very sad really. Despite the money they must earn, what is actually going on inside their heads? Nick Read, the current CEO, was responsible for large bonuses being paid to the board and staff below the board, just for co-operating with the inquiry.

When this was discovered and heavily criticised, Nick Read said that he felt that people needed incentivising.

Incentivising? Oh dear god.

Documents found by the inquiry indicated that Sir Wyn Williams had given his blessing to these bonuses. This was completely false. How had it even been written into official Post Office documents that he had personally agreed the bonuses? It was fabricated by someone. The calibre of the people in these positions is truly questionable.

This mentality is repeated throughout the organisation with names of roles such as these: Executive Social Media Architect or Executive Relationship Managers, who apparently are tasked with being the "friendly face of the company, always **making sure everyone feels valued and appreciated**". Hello? I thought this was a day job not a kindergarten!

I even heard someone from the Post Office executive board during his appearance at the inquiry say they had signs up in the offices saying, "Be good to each other" and "Make this a great place to work". These are the sort of wall posters we had at primary school, yet these are grown adults who are apparently the top-end of executives.

I repeat, these are the people who were responsible for ruining so many lives

Bloody useless

But, ladies and gentlemen, this is the rub. The "high level talent" these C-suite titles are aimed at, is a folly. For what has been revealed at the inquiry is that many of these elite executives didn't have a clue what they were doing or why they were even doing it. Their skillsets revealed as very narrow.

I'm struggling to suggest this is common in all firms but a lot of the witnesses that came from external firms, not just the Post Office, were of this same calibre so it does appear to be endemic. In particular, the Post Office did seem to be the worst for this.

Many of the top people were recruited with absolutely no experience of the job they were being offered.

Head of Criminal Law at the Post Office, Chris Connolly, had no formal legal qualifications. He was not legally qualified, yet he held a senior position overseeing criminal prosecutions.

Former head of criminal law, Jarnail Singh, was also found to have no qualifications in criminal law and ran a private practice alongside his Post Office role.

The inquiry highlighted that Hugh Flemington, the former head of legal, had limited experience in criminal law and relied heavily on Jarnail Singh.

Head of Auditing, Helen Rose, admitted she had no training or formal qualifications in the process of auditing whatsoever. Despite this, she conducted audits that led to serious consequences for sub-postmasters. Specifically, the case of Lee Castleton OBE.

Investigators that attended post office branches to investigate discrepancies were not trained in investigating, were not familiar the Horizon IT system and as such did no investigating at all.

Richard Callard, who served as the government's representative on the Post Office board between 2014 and 2018, had no previous experience or training as a director and felt overwhelmed by his responsibilities.

As we can see these are not isolated incidents, all were on very large salaries paid out of public funds.

How could this happen or be deemed acceptable for any reason? In any previous employment of mine, actual relevant skills were imperative, obviously. Nothing like this could have possibly happened. It's incredible on any level.

More corporate folly

Nonexecutive directors or NEDs were devoting two days a fortnight to Post Office business for very large fees and when questioned about this at the inquiry, all of them thought it was easily enough time.

Some are NEDs for many different companies at the same time. One was actively trying to reduce his time devoted to the Post Office to two days a month despite the mess the entire company was in.

There are many more examples of this incredible situation. Perhaps it's because it's a public company using unlimited public funds. Maybe because there is no personal risk whatsoever, everything, including the recruitment policy, is either low quality or, as I suspect, just a kind of nepotism of hand-picking individual people already known and who are easily manipulated. It really is dumbfounding.

The board didn't seem to know what was really going on because they were not told things by those below them and information that should have reached the board, didn't. So what were they actually doing? Not as much as one would expect.

They didn't actively seek out the reality of operations, they just relied on hearsay and PR strap lines. The whole top level of the organisation behaved in a completely dysfunctional way. How?

How can this happen at the highest level of such a large public company, with people who somehow live their working lives believing they are "talented" and are receiving huge salaries from the public purse, amounts that are eye watering to most people.

Teams don't communicate with each other

The Post Office is also made up of enormous amounts of "teams". These teams also seemed to need their own support teams, such as the Executive Correspondence team and its support team. Does the correspondence team need a support team? Wow, really? Technical level 1 team, level 2 team, level 3 team, level 4 team and their associated support teams. But comically, these teams don't communicate with each other.

The inquiry revealed that when a postmaster phoned the helpline with a problem, it was passed to various technical support levels before being generally abandoned and closed as an issue, not passed onto the "team" that should be dealing with it, leaving the postmaster in total limbo, with no proper communication. Just appalling.

Some teams avoided communicating with each other. There is rivalry between teams, and some don't get on with each other. These are grown adults. How could anyone with any kind of normal personality behave like this?

How an individual can be so personally ingrained with a job role, when it's not even their own business and then behave so childishly towards other people, is totally beyond me. I'm certain they would not behave like this if they were running their own business. They would never take that risk.

It was revealed that very many of these teams were dysfunctional. It's simply not common sense. To me it is beyond my comprehension that this situation exists, but the Public Inquiry revealed that it really does. Not isolated instances but virtually accepted company norms.

An example, take the Jarnail Singh, he was also head of prosecutions for the entire Post Office Ltd. According to his testimony at the Inquiry, not once in his 20-year career of overseeing prosecutions of sub postmasters did he or his "team" ever have any communication with the "investigators" and lawyers putting the cases together! I mean…..WTF !

Despite prosecutions ramping up year on year, he never once thought he should inquire for himself, just out of professional interest, what was occurring to cause so many postmasters to require prosecuting.

It didn't cross his mind to maybe speak to the managers of the staff manning the helplines that postmasters were telephoning with their complaints. He had absolutely no idea whatsoever of any of the problems postmasters were battling with, or how they were being investigated or what the actual outcome was.

Showing no interest in the potential safety of all these prosecutions, he just blundered on and got on with prosecuting. When questioned about this at the inquiry he merely said that it wasn't his job to inquire into anything like that.

Asked if he could see any problems with that, he couldn't. Astonishing.

I'm sure their job title impresses their wives and girlfriends, and the salary is fabulous but in reality, they seem woeful at the job.

As a convicted postmaster this is very hard to swallow, their "group think" incompetency ruined so many lives. This type of mentality certainly ruined my life. I repeat, the actual skill sets of all these types seem very narrow. A move slightly out of their usual range and they are a fish out of water. It seems many could not boil an egg.

What a situation. I think the public believe that these large corporations are staffed by experts in their field. The inquiry has revealed this to be far from reality.

Not to get too philosophical, but in my view, this is also a hollow way to live. It's a kind of pretence that would be deeply unsatisfying to me. They really do live in a bubble, an echo chamber packed with group-thinking, like-minded replicas simply repeating themselves. Giving up a third of your life to spend it like this is tragic. I'm so glad I am nothing like this.

Outside of this protection I doubt they could survive in the real world; they have been working like this for so long it's the sum total of all they could ever do.

Outsourcing

The higher up the organisation these teams are, the more they appear to outsource their roles to external agencies. From evidence heard at the inquiry, despite having a sizeable permanent in-house legal team, the Post Office's legal department outsourced almost everything to external legal firms at enormous public expense.

Even the "Director of communications" employed

external PR firms on monthly retainers to provide him with straplines for media press releases. Jason Beer KC, Counsel to the inquiry, was astonished at the sheer amount of outsourcing the Post Office used for decisions and reviews.

When he asked various witnesses from these departments if they could see the clear problem with this, again, none of them could. Again, this is the kind of "group think" they all display.

The best was saved till last. Nigel Railton, brought in as the latest interim chair, was questioned at the inquiry. He was asked what he intended to do in his new role.

He explained that he had been head hunted from Camelot and was in the process of doing a complete strategic review of the whole business, to enable him to recommend to the board the changes he believed needed to be implemented.

When asked what his review consisted of and where it was up to, he explained he had outsourced the entire strategic review to an external firm and was in the process of waiting for their final analysis and report. Just astonishing. The house cat could do that.

If the Chairman's only plan is to outsource his job to someone else, why does he even exist? The Post Office seems to have become an organisation that exists purely to sustain itself, wasting public money while refusing to take responsibility for anything. What didn't they outsource?

This is the reality of life at the top. For me, given the circumstances, all this holds no respect. The entire organisation continues to be operating as hopeless in every single area. No matter who comes and goes, there is no common sense, no practical skillsets and a strangely-out-of-touch-with-reality mindset.

I am personally a fan of the writer Charles Bukowski and this classic comment from him about the drudgery of corporate life sums everything up,

'How the hell could a person enjoy being awakened at 6.30am, leap out of bed, dress, force-feed, shit, piss, brush teeth and hair, then fight the traffic. To get to a place where essentially you make lots of money for somebody else and are asked to be grateful for the opportunity to do so. The corporate life leads to stupidity. Robots live better lives than cubicle employees, don't do it, it's a trap'.

Government involvement

Government ministers, relying on assurances from Post Office executives, misled Parliament about Horizon's reliability. For instance, in 2015, Minister George Freeman read a speech asserting Horizon's reliability, based on information received from Post Office CEO Paula Vennells, despite growing evidence to the contrary.

Successive governments used the excuse that the Post Office was an "Arms-Length Business" (ALB) to wash their hands of responsibility. But the reality? Every Post Office board **always** included a government representative, and they **signed off on every major decision,** including the attempt at derailing the GLO and all the enormous legal costs for crushing innocent postmasters in court. The Business Secretary at the time of my prosecution, Peter Mandelson, did nothing. His successors Vince Cable, Sajid Javid, Greg Clark, all had the power to intervene. None did. Instead, they bankrolled the Post Office's legal fight, using taxpayer money to continue to persecute innocent people.

As a citizen, wronged by a public company, it has become clear that the government are not on your side. They did everything to avoid any responsibility, just like many previous scandals, Hillsborough for instance. They would rather facilitate a wholesale cover up than find out the truth.

This is an appalling state of affairs. From the country with the historic reputation of fairness, due process and the rule of law. It just ain't true. Perhaps never was. A myth.

A startling fact was revealed

One fact that this inquiry revealed about my circumstances over the years was the reason the Post Office never pursued me for the shortfall at my branch. It was revealed that after my conviction for false accounting, I was top of their list for civil recovery of the shortfall of just over £44,000. This despite the fact there was no evidence of theft and the failed proceeds of crime application against me.

Back in 2010 the early legal team Shoosmiths, wrote to Post Office stating that if they issued a civil action against me, my defence would be that the Horizon system was not reliable and no proper investigation of the cause of the shortfall was undertaken. Way ahead of the curve it turns out!

So of course, the Post Office did not want to open that can of worms and never pursued it. They were pursuing individuals who they felt were in the weakest position whilst weaving around others who may mention Horizon.

I never knew the reason they didn't come after me until the inquiry. Incredible

The inquiry comes to an end

The end of the inquiry was bittersweet. We were glad it was all over, it had consumed a lot of our time over the three years it took to complete. Sometimes riveting, sometimes bogged down with legalese. We were both sick of watching it live on YouTube every day. Truly jaded with it but felt compelled to watch. Witnessing some truly heartbreaking stories and a procession of awful individuals responsible for the tragedy.

Our trips down to London to appear in person, staying in hotels near to the location of the inquiry, have been both enjoyable and stressful. We were present for the last day in London, but we also knew that this would probably be the last time all the people we had met over the period of this nightmare would be together in the same place.

I struck up a lovely friendship with the great Lee Castleton OBE, for instance. He has been one of the stalwarts throughout this tragedy. A lovely fella through and through, so I know I will miss him. Tim Moloney KC representing Hudgells solicitors throughout the inquiry has become a friend too. His take down of Paula Vennells at her appearance has gone down in history.

Too many people to mention. This has affected so many. Everything has been such a long slog, everything.

18

Bates v The Post Office

On New Year's Day 2024 a moment we had hoped for years finally arrived, the scandal we had lived through was now unfolding on millions of TV screens across Britain.

Donna and I sat in front of the television, not knowing what to expect. Would it do justice to the scale of our suffering? Would it capture the sheer madness of what had happened? At first, we both thought it was light on details, but then we realised, the true power of it wasn't in the details, they actually got it dead right. They showed the scale of the visceral impact it has had on peoples' lives. And it worked.

The public finally got it. Overnight, everything changed. The response the next day was incredible. Just unbelievable.

Social media exploded. I had many messages of support on Facebook and twitter. People were stopping me in Tesco with kind words of support.

Friends, strangers, journalists, all wanting to talk about it. Twitter was flooded with outrage. "How the hell did this happen? People went to prison for this? Why aren't the Post Office bosses in jail?" It felt surreal. For years we had been screaming into the void, ignored by many politicians and the national press. Now, suddenly, it was all anyone was talking about it.

My phone was ringing off the hook with requests from the BBC, ITV and many radio stations to appear and talk about my experiences. The scandal became headlines every night on every channel. We couldn't believe it. Suddenly thrust into the national psyche it felt like a living dream. From the ridiculous to the sublime.

It had barely made much of an impression in the press for all the preceding decades. Despite Nick Wallis' huge attempts to keep it from sinking. There had always been something to push it down the league of importance. General elections, Brexit, the pandemic, etc. Now it was of national importance.

Of course, now that the scandal was dominating every front page, the government had to act. Rishi Sunak came out and announced that they would quash the remaining convictions en masse. A noble gesture? No, It was **forced**. For years, every government had shrugged off every plea for justice, hiding behind the excuse that the Post Office was an "arm's-length business". Now, with the public breathing down their necks, they had no choice but to do something.

The real question was, why did it take a TV drama to force their hand? Something is clearly wrong with how things are usually dealt with.

The BBC

I am invited onto BBC breakfast with Jon Kaye and Sally Nugent. At 6:45 am a BBC car arrived to pick me up. Donna came with me; we both knew this was a big moment. Media City in Salford was eerily quiet at that hour and when we stepped inside it felt strangely empty. No bustling newsroom or busy people rushing around.

There are eight other affected sub-postmasters there too and it's going to be a communal interview with us all at once.

We were taken into a room to discuss with the producer what was generally going to happen. The atmosphere was unreal. None of us could believe how this had been catapulted onto National TV overnight. Everybody was very friendly and there was a really pleasant feel to the place. Tea and biscuits were flowing!

I was called for my turn in "hair and make-up". They realised there is very little they can do with me, so I am back out after about one minute.

I didn't feel nervous at all. Probably because it all felt slightly surreal. There is nobody there actually watching. Just the ancillary staff helping us through the general procedure before doing it. We are then led onto the set ready for the live broadcast.

Before the broadcast started, Sally says to me "don't worry, there are only seven million people watching". Strangely it didn't feel like that at all. There were no camera operators, we are in an empty studio just with the presenters. This all felt very relaxed. I think we all felt that this was a turning point.

Link to the BBC special
https://www.youtube.com/watch?v=E_eFfJWL7WY&t=30s

We are live on BBC breakfast for an hour, straight after this we are then whisked into BBC Radio 5 live studios for another interview and phone in, hosted by Nicky Campbell. The response is staggering, many people phoning in with their own tales of being caught up in the scandal but they had never spoken about it to anybody until the TV drama was aired. It was all quite emotional to be honest.

As I am leaving the BBC building, there are people from ITV waiting for me. I had a taxi waiting to take us home so I couldn't go over to their studios to do the same thing. They asked if people could come to my house. We agreed to this and off we went.

About an hour after arriving home the people from ITV arrived and we conduct another interview. Of course we go over the same things. Seems a bit daft in your own house but all goes well and they leave after a couple of hours. It's all a bit of a whirlwind. We are so happy that this whole issue has been projected into this high-profile national subject at last. It should have been years ago, but I believe that the UK public are simply used to scandal after scandal, pension mis-selling, mortgage mis-selling, Grenfell tower, Windrush, Hillsborough, Infected blood etc, so it just blows over relatively unnoticed.

I have personally done quite a few interviews and media appearances since, but I have decided I'm not doing any more. I don't want to be the face of this scandal. There are others who are far, far better at it than me. I am prepared to do some radio, especially if it's for Nick Wallis, but as for the TV, I don't want to do anymore. Plus, I look like that gonk every time! Having said this, I may do one last TV appearance after the Inquiry reports its conclusions. If I am invited to of course.

While the publicity has been incredibly beneficial for many reasons, it has not changed the behaviour of the Post Office or its law firms. They still operate in an insulting way to the postmasters. I did not expect any different.
Despite everything, the Post Office and their legal teams haven't changed. The same dirty tactics, the same stonewalling, the same adversarial behaviour. Nothing has shifted including their PR strategy.

Sir Wyn Williams, chair of the inquiry, explicitly said these methods had "no place" in a compensation scheme. Yet they continue, because this is what they do. These people aren't interested in justice, they're interested in their personal fees. How do they sleep at night? The answer is, they don't care.

And frankly, I no longer care what happens to them either. AI is coming for them, and they will be obsolete long before they see it coming. When that day comes, expect no sympathy from me

I wonder what their children think of them.

I personally believe it's clear the Post Office as an organisation is in terminal decline and has been for many years. It has a bloated management structure not based in reality. It hasn't made a profit for decades. It's propped up by huge government subsidy every year. A large proportion of the services a post office branch offers is available online. It's almost exclusively mail only and there are many superior firms doing that very thing. It's a dead duck. It will surely disappear from the high street almost unnoticed over time. It may be a place the local community once called a hub, but surely that is seriously insufficient for it to survive.

This is just my opinion. I'm sure there are many current postmasters who might disagree entirely, but I have certainly seen a huge change on the high street. Things are just not the same as they were. It's a shame.

On a personal level, since the day I was convicted, I have not set foot in a Post Office. I never will. I cannot stand to even see the vans driving around.

19

The heroes

The are many people who without their interest and work, there would be nothing. Fighting a public institution with bottomless pockets backed by the government is an almost impossible task. Some individuals have made all the difference and pretty much against all odds.

Sir Alan Bates

I don't need to say anything about Alan. His role in all this has been widely reported. Without him, nothing would have happened to right this enormous wrong.

Nick Wallis

Nick has been involved since 2010 when a chance conversation with a taxi driver who told him his pregnant wife had been sent to prison for a crime she hadn't committed, alerted his journalistic instincts to find out more.

His subsequent work has been of crucial importance in

uncovering the truth about the whole scandal. He never missed a beat or allowed his determination to drop for the next 15 years. I first noticed him when he kept popping up on TV talking about the plight that some postmasters he had met were in. For me, personally, this was the first glimmer of hope. He has done so much work behind the scenes, it's too much to list.

When The GLO started he was able to tweet out every single word of the trials live on his twitter feed. This was of huge importance. This was an enormous window into the trials which captivated many, many interested people, primarily the affected postmasters of course. Every day I was hooked, watching his live feed.

His personal commentary was both entertaining and useful for us to understand some of the legal jargon and bogged down technicalities of the proceedings. Not having to wait until law firms sent sporadic simplified briefings of what had been going on was a godsend. The dedication he has shown to this whole story has been incredible.

Thank you so much Nick

He has written the definitive book about the whole scandal in great detail. Nobody knows or will ever know more than

Nick Wallis about this subject.

Nick is also a brilliant personality, incredibly approachable, easy going and I now consider him a friend.

He has also undertaken a national tour of the UK to promote his book 'The Great Post Office scandal' and I was honoured to be invited by him to appear on stage at the Crewe Lyceum on 13th April 2024. I was joined on stage by my brother Steve for the show. It was very well attended.

James Arbuthnot

Lord Arbuthnot has been, without doubt, a shining light in this awful scandal. His high profile and widely respected position in Parliament have been crucial to this entire scandal eventually being uncovered. I have mentioned his role earlier in this book, but it bears repeating. He has used his authority to incredible effect to personally help the plight of the sub-postmasters, demanding investigations and accountability. He was instrumental in calling for an independent review into the Post Office's actions and played a role in securing the public inquiry. He has advocated forcefully for fair compensation to all those affected. He really deserves special recognition for his actions. A true champion for all sub-postmasters.

Ron Warmington and Ian Henderson

These two amazing chaps are the people behind Second Sight. The forensic accountants who started to unpick the appalling conduct of the Post Office. They were on to so many things that the Post Office had done wrong and uncovered some of the actual faults in the Horizon system. No wonder Post Office froze them out. They were uncovering too much. They also risked their reputation by not shutting up about it for many, many years. Despite being silenced by the Post Office they played a pivotal role in proving the scandal was a systemic failure and not individual wrongdoing. Their findings were crucial in securing justice for all the sub-postmasters. Heroes.

Paul Marshall representing

Seema Misra, Janet Skinner and Tracey Felstead

Without Paul, Seema, Janet and Tracey, the overturning of convictions would have only been on one count. **That a fair trial was impossible.** All the other law firms were pushing not to go for the second count, **that it was an abuse of process and an affront to public conscience**

for the appellants to have even faced prosecution. This was absolutely crucial. Not only did this succeed, but it also then applied to all the other convicted sub-postmasters. I'm still at a loss as to why the other law firms, including mine, were adamant to not go for both counts. This ruling meant that the Public Inquiry had to become statutory and gave us so much more clout to go for far higher compensation. Despite this, the Post Office are still "not admitting liability".

Karl Flinders Computer Weekly

Karl has continually written dozens of articles in Computer Weekly since Rebecca Thomson first wrote about it in 2009. He has consistently been on top of everything that has happened since then and is a real friend and source of knowledge about everything to do with the scandal. He has extensively interviewed many wrongfully prosecuted postmasters sharing their personal experiences and struggles. His persistence has helped ensure this story has not been forgotten.

Tim McCormack

A former postmaster, Tim emerged as a prominent campaigner during this scandal. Using his background in computer programming and analysis, he played a pivotal role in challenging the Post Office's narrative. He contacted Paula Vennells directly asserting he had clear evidence of an intermittent bug that could cause financial discrepancies. The Post Office tried to dismiss his assertions, but the Public Inquiry showed that Tim was regularly quoted in internal documents. He was under their skin. He made a huge difference.

Eleanor Shaikh

Eleanor has been a dedicated campaigner who has played a significant role in advocating for justice in this scandal. Utilising the Freedom of Information Act she has submitted numerous requests that have uncovered critical documents related to the scandal. Her incredible unwavering commitment has also contributed to the overlooked impact of the scandal on the children of affected sub-postmasters.

Christopher Head OBE

Christopher was the Uk's youngest postmaster and was swept up with the scandal when he also encountered discrepancies at his branch. In recognition of his relentless advocacy, he was awarded an OBE in the 2025 new year's honours list. His tireless work on behalf of all the postmasters has been rightfully acknowledged.

Lee Castleton

Lee has been another tireless campaigner. In recognition of his efforts to seek justice for himself and other victims, Castleton was awarded an OBE in the 2025 New Year Honours. He expressed hope that this honour would help maintain public awareness of the ongoing issues surrounding the scandal. Lee remains committed to advocating for full accountability and compensation for all affected sub postmasters. His own legal action seeks not only personal vindication but also aims to set a precedent for others seeking justice in the wake of the Horizon scandal.

Steve Darlington

Without his support and help through the early days I would not have been able to cope with all the things that I had to face. I had to lean on him heavily as this all unfolded and his calm expertise and practical mindset saw me through so many things I cannot list them all. It was a very difficult situation to say the least. He contributed untold numbers of hours during the mediation period for many different postmasters, all for no pay.

His further involvement is highlighted in a communication dated 13th June 2014 where he addresses concerns regarding Post Office non-disclosure of system generated transactions and Horizon's integrity. In an email to the Post Office he emphasised the critical significance of the "Helen Rose report" which detailed potential flaws in the Horizon system. This email was discussed at length during the Public Inquiry. He has made a difference.
I will never be able to repay the dedication Steve has shown.

Where am I now?

The toll this has taken on myself and my partner Donna has been immeasurable. It's been so many years.

So many years we should have been doing the things we enjoy, not embroiled in the struggle that this has been. It has robbed us of an incredible amount of time.

Despite this inescapable fact, we have managed to keep ourselves together both physically and mentally. But no amount of compensation due can ever buy this time back.

Even £100 million would not make the slightest difference to that.

I have been diagnosed with PTSD and depression. This has been with me for many years and still is.

As I have said, this has affected people around me. My brother Steve has had to worry about all this for me, despite having enough in his own life to think about! My ex-partner has had the long-term burden of this too, having to bring up my daughter with very little financial help from me because of the terrible circumstances I was thrown into. It's not been easy for her.

My father has had the worry of witnessing me in all this trouble. He is approaching 88 now and it's still not quite over.

The compensation that everybody knows we are due has been a complex situation too. Incredibly, the Post Office oversee the scheme I am in. The people who ruined so many lives like mine are the ones deciding the amount we should be receiving. It's atrocious but true. We all know that the Government pull the stings

I have had to endure many hours of psychological

assessments just to show the Post Office the mental state I've been left in. I am to receive weekly counselling for at least 18 months to help me get back to something approaching how I used to be. It has taken Hudgells Solicitors a long time to finally get my entire claim together because it has clearly been complicated. This has now been presented to The Post Office but as of today I have yet to receive an "offer" from them. Hardly anybody has settled fully with the Post Office.

They are still treating us in an aggressive way by offering very low amounts. It really is an insult that they would do this, but not surprising. Ultimately the current government are the people in charge because the taxpayer will be footing the bill, not the Post Office. Can any government be trusted? No, of course not.

I *have* received interim payments which have taken the immediate financial stress away and this has helped, but until this is finally over, we still cannot put it behind us.

We cannot wait for that day. We've been waiting so long. Even then, this is going to take some getting over, for both of us. Luckily, we are as strong together as we have ever been, and that really bodes well for our future.

Final Reflections

My story is part of the greatest miscarriage of justice in British history. It exposed corruption, incompetence, and the utter disregard for human lives by a public institution that should have served and protected those it employed. It has taken decades to uncover the truth, and for many, justice has come far too late.

Even now, as this book comes to an end, stupid battles are still being fought with stupid people.

The Post Office continues to resist full accountability, legal firms still act aggressively in the Post Office's interests, another aberration, and compensation is being dragged out as long as possible. This is hard to understand.

But despite all of this, there is one thing the Post Office and its enablers failed to crush: our resilience.

This isn't just a story of injustice. It's a story of resistance.

Signed Sealed Destroyed

Steve and me.

At the time of writing this book, I have spent 16 years of my life fighting for justice. Despite the enormous publicity and outrage from the public, I have still not received my final compensation and face 12 to 18 months of professional counselling and therapy for PTSD.

This has been a very long road.

Signed Sealed Destroyed